FOREIGN AFFAIRS
Special Collection

OPTIONS FOR THE UNITED STATES

Foreign Affairs Special Collection: Iran and the Bomb 2

Editor Gideon Rose Introduces the Collection

View the video at www.foreignaffairs.com/iran-video-introduction.

There is no more controversial issue on the foreign policy agenda than how to deal with Iran's nuclear program, especially now that direct negotiations have resulted in an interim accord between Iran and the P5+1. Whether diplomacy ultimately succeeds or fails—and what the consequences will be in either case—will be among 2014's most gripping dramas.

ON IRANIAN POLITICS
"Who is Ali Khamenei?" by Iranian dissident Akbar Ganji, is a ground-breaking intellectual profile of Iran's enigmatic supreme leader.

ON NEGOTIATIONS
Robert Jervis' "Getting to Yes With Iran" sets out a strategy for effective coercive diplomacy. A follow-on article evaluates how well the Obama administration has performed so far.

ON THE UNITED STATES
Matthew Kroenig's "Still Time to Attack Iran" advocates taking the bull by the horns and launching a limited U.S. military strike against Iranian nuclear targets.

ON ISRAEL
In "Pushing Peace," Trita Parsi takes on those who say that nuclear negotiations are bad for Israel.

Visit ForeignAffairs.com for more on these topics—and all our other great content.

Introduction

Gideon Rose

There is no more controversial issue on the foreign policy agenda than how to deal with Iran's nuclear program. A year and a half ago, we published *Iran and the Bomb*, containing highlights from three decades of our coverage on the topic. Since then, the issue has remained on the world's front burner, with the direct negotiations begun last fall marking a new era of diplomatic progress. Supporters of the interim accord between Iran and the P5+1 countries (China, France, Germany, Russia, the United Kingdom, and the United States) consider the agreement a landmark event paving the way for an end to one of the world's most enduring and volatile conflicts. Many critics take the opposite view, seeing it as a modern-day Munich paving the way for an eventual nuclear Iran. Whether the negotiations will succeed or fail, and what the consequences will be in either case, will be among 2014's most gripping dramas.

As usual, *Foreign Affairs* has been at the center of public debate over these events, and with the negotiations coming to a head, we have decided to publish an update to our earlier collection, pulling together a broad range of pieces from the last year that illuminate Iran's turn toward negotiations, the pros and cons of the interim agreement, and the geopolitical and psychological intricacies of the crucial U.S.-Iranian-Israeli triangle. Once again, the authors include world-renowned experts from several disciplines and professional backgrounds, and once again their arguments span every significant position on the political spectrum. Now, as before, therefore, the collection offers an excellent overview of the current

GIDEON ROSE is Editor of *Foreign Affairs*.

situation and all the material required for readers to develop their own opinions about how to proceed.

The first section of the book contains articles examining the inner workings of the Iranian regime. "Who Is Ali Khamenei?" by the Iranian dissident Akbar Ganji, is a groundbreaking intellectual profile of Iran's enigmatic supreme leader, the single most important decision-maker in the entire affair. Suzanne Maloney's "Why Rouhani Won—And Why Khamenei Let Him" stresses just how much of a hand Khamenei had in the election of the reformer Hassan Rouhani as president last June, and what that means for the chances of real change in the Islamic Republic. And in "Rouhani's Gorbachev Moment," Stephen Kotkin explores how one will be able to tell whether Rouhani is a genuine reformer or not.

The second section looks at the recent negotiations and interim accord. Robert Jervis' "Getting to Yes With Iran" sets out a strategy for effective coercive diplomacy, and his follow-on article, "On the Road to Yes With Iran," evaluates how well the Obama administration has performed on that front so far. In "Talk Is Cheap," Patrick Clawson warns that getting Iran to come to the negotiating table was easy, but that maintaining its interest in talks will be much harder. Finally, in "Saved by the Deal," Suzanne Maloney urges patience on the grounds that nuclear diplomacy has already started to empower Iran's moderates and, should it continue, will intensify the "pressure on them to deliver to the Iranian people."

The third section sets out alternative policy options for the United States. In "Don't Get Suckered by Iran," Mitchell B. Reiss and Ray Takeyh call on the United States to try to fix the interim agreement's shortfalls, including its promise to eventually treat Iran's nuclear program "in the same manner as that of any other non-nuclear weapon state party to the NPT." In "Confidence Enrichment," Kenneth Pollack explains why the interim agreement is a deal worth taking. Matthew Kroenig's "Still Time to Attack Iran" advocates taking the bull by the horns and launching a limited U.S. military strike against Iranian nuclear targets. Colin Kahl responds that it is "Still Not Time to Attack Iran," since a military strike would cause more problems than it would solve. And in "Befriend the Scientists," Jacques E. C. Hymans writes that, for the nuclear deal to stick, the United States must win over the scientists and pencil pushers who keep Iran's nuclear program running.

The fourth and last section of the book widens the discussion, bringing in voices from Israel. In "Pushing Peace," Trita Parsi takes on those who say that nuclear negotiations are bad for Israel. Elliott Abrams assumes the opposite stance in "Bibi the Bad Cop," explaining what Israel could try to do to thwart talks. And in "Why Israel Is So Afraid," Ariel Ilan Roth writes that Washington's diplomatic engagement with Tehran may, ironically, make Jerusalem more likely to attack now, because it fears that later could be too late.

In my introduction to our earlier collection, I noted that the challenge in Iran policy (as is so often the case) lay not in picking an ideal course but in choosing among lesser evils. That remains true today: Practically nobody thinks that the interim agreement represents a wonderful, durable solution to the problem of Iran's nuclear file. The real question is whether it can serve as a useful platform for further negotiations, a confidence-building measure that allows the parties to test one another's sincerity and ability to deliver more substantive results down the road. Jaw-jaw, Churchill famously said, is better than war-war—but whether this current round of jaw-jaw will prove a substitute for war-war, or merely a prelude to it, remains an open question. ❧

Who Is Ali Khamenei?

The Worldview of Iran's Supreme Leader

Akbar Ganji

In June, Hassan Rouhani was elected president of the Islamic Republic of Iran. Rouhani ran as a reform candidate, and many have interpreted his victory as a harbinger of a possible liberalization or rationalization of Iranian domestic and foreign policy. But the dominant figure in Iranian politics is not the president but rather the supreme leader, Ayatollah Ali Khamenei. The Iranian constitution endows the supreme leader with tremendous authority over all major state institutions, and Khamenei, who has held the post since 1989, has found many other ways to further increase his influence. Formally or not, the executive, legislative, and judicial branches of the government all operate under his absolute sovereignty; Khamenei is Iran's head of state, commander in chief, and top ideologue. His views are what will ultimately shape Iranian policy, and so it is worth exploring them in detail.

Khamenei was born in the northeastern Iranian city of Mashhad in 1939. His father was a religious scholar of modest means, and Khamenei, the second of eight children, followed his father's path to seminary. (Two of his brothers are also clerics.) He studied in Qom from 1958 to 1964, and while there, he joined the religious opposition movement of Ayatollah Ruhollah Khomeini, in 1962.

AKBAR GANJI is an Iranian journalist and dissident. He was imprisoned in Tehran from 2000 to 2006, and his writings are currently banned in Iran. This article was translated from the Farsi by Evan Siegel.

He played an important role in the 1979 Iranian Revolution and went on to become Iran's president, from 1981 to 1989, and then Khomeini's successor as supreme leader.

Khamenei has always been in contact with the world of Iranian intellectuals, and the basic outlines of his thinking were laid down in his youth and young adulthood, during the 1950s and 1960s. Iran was then a monarchy and an ally of the United States; according to the Iranian opposition at the time, the shah was nothing but an American puppet. Unlike many other Islamists, Khamenei had contact with the most important secular opposition intellectuals and absorbed their prerevolutionary discourse. But he was also a seminary student, whose chief focus was learning sharia, Islamic law. He became acquainted with the theoreticians of the Muslim Brotherhood and was influenced by the works of Sayyid Qutb, some of which Khamenei himself translated into Persian.

As a young man, Khamenei saw a tension between the West and the Third World, and these views hardened during his dealings with the United States after the Iranian Revolution. He concluded that Washington was determined to overthrow the Islamic Republic and that all other issues raised by U.S. officials were nothing more than smoke screens. Even today, he believes that the U.S. government is bent on regime change in Iran, whether through internal collapse, democratic revolution, economic pressure, or military invasion.

Khamenei has always been critical of liberal democracy and thinks that capitalism and the West are in inevitable long-term decline. Moreover, he sees Washington as inherently Islamophobic. Nevertheless, he is not reflexively anti-Western or anti-American. He does not believe that the United States and the West are responsible for all of the Islamic world's problems, that they must be destroyed, or that the Koran and sharia are by themselves sufficient to address the needs of the modern world. He considers science and progress to be "Western civilization's truth," and he wants the Iranian people to learn this truth. He is not a crazy, irrational, or reckless zealot searching for opportunities for aggression. But his deep-rooted views and intransigence are bound to make any negotiations with the West difficult and protracted, and any serious improvement in the relationship between Iran and the United States will have to be part of a major comprehensive deal involving significant concessions on both sides.

A PORTRAIT OF THE SUPREME LEADER AS A YOUNG MAN

To understand Khamenei's worldview, it helps to start by looking at the history of U.S. intervention in Iran. In 1953, the Eisenhower administration helped engineer a coup against the democratically elected government of Mohammad Mosaddeq, and Washington was the chief supporter of Mohammad Reza Shah Pahlavi's authoritarian regime, until its overthrow in 1979. This helped shape the discourse of all of the regime's opponents; opposition to the shah went hand in hand with opposition to the United States, since the shah was considered Washington's gendarme.

Khamenei was 40 when the revolution occurred; before then, he had been a seminary student and cleric, but one engaged with the broader world as well as his narrow religious circles. As he said in a meeting with ulama (Muslim scholars) and young clergymen in May 2012, "I participated in intellectual circles before the revolution and had close relations with political groups. I got to know them all, and got into discussions and debates with many of them." He was a man of music, poetry, and novels as well as religious law. No other present-day *marja* (senior ayatollah) or prominent *faqih* (Islamic jurist) has such a cosmopolitan past.

Khamenei's widespread relationships with secular intellectuals in Iran radicalized his views about the United States, since these circles became increasingly anti-American after the 1953 coup and the U.S. backing of the shah and his subsequent repression of dissidents. As Khamenei's friend Mehdi Akhavan Sales, a poet, put it in one of his verses, "I will not forget: that we were a flame, and they doused us with water." Khamenei has spoken about the U.S. role in the 1953 coup several times, and the memory continues to resonate with him today. As he said just last year in a meeting with university students in Tehran,

> It is interesting to realize that America overthrew his government even though Mosaddeq had shown no animosity toward them. He had stood up to the British and trusted the Americans. He had hoped that the Americans would help him; he had friendly relations with them, he expressed an interest in them, perhaps he [even] expressed humility toward them. And [still] the Americans [overthrew] such a government. It was not as if the government in power in Tehran had been anti-American. No, it had been friendly toward them. But the interests of Arrogance [a term Khamenei often uses to symbolize the United States] required that the Americans ally with the British. They gathered money and brought it here and did their job. Then, when they brought their coup into fruition and had returned the shah, who had fled, they had the run of the country.

Khamenei had strong ties to Jalal Al-e Ahmad and Ali Shariati, the two most influential intellectuals of the prerevolutionary period. They were important contributors to the theory of "Westoxication." But anti-imperialism seems to have been the strand of secular intellectual thought that shaped Khamenei the most.

In prerevolutionary Iranian opposition intellectual circles, Western culture and civilization were not only disparaged as a model but considered to be in crisis and decline. The Third World was its rising alternative; as the Iranian writer Daryush Ashuri, a contemporary of Khamenei, put it, "The Third World is composed of the poor and colonized nations, which are at the same time revolutionary." Iran was ostensibly independent, but colonialism was seen as taking a new form there, with native ruling political elites serving as agents of imperialism and working to secure its interests. The Western world, led by the United States, moreover, was thought to be laying the groundwork for its political and economic expansion by destroying indigenous cultures. Under such circumstances, it was easy to see Islam as not simply a religion but also a cultural and ideological weapon in the struggle against imperialism.

As a young man, Khamenei loved novels. He read such Iranian writers as Muhammad Ali Jamalzadah, Sadeq Chubak, and Sadeq Hedayat but came to feel that they paled before classic Western writers from France, Russia, and the United Kingdom. He has praised Leo Tolstoy and Mikhail Sholokhov and likes Honoré de Balzac and Michel Zévaco, but he considers Victor Hugo supreme. As he told some officials of Iran's state-run television network in 2004,

> In my opinion, Victor Hugo's *Les Misérables* is the best novel that has been written in history. I have not read all the novels written throughout history, no doubt, but I have read many that relate to the events of various centuries. I have read some very old novels. For example, say, I've read *The Divine Comedy*. I have read *Amir Arsalan*. I have also read *A Thousand and One Nights*. . . . [But] *Les Misérables* is a miracle in the world of novel writing. . . . I have said over and over again, go read *Les Misérables* once. This *Les Misérables* is a book of sociology, a book of history, a book of criticism, a divine book, a book of love and feeling.

Khamenei felt that novels gave him insight into the deeper realities of life in the West. "Read the novels of some authors with leftist tendencies, such as Howard Fast," he advised an audience of writers and artists in 1996. "Read the famous book *The Grapes of Wrath*, written by John Steinbeck, . . . and see what it says about the situation of the left and how the capitalists of the so-called center of democracy treated them." He is also a fan of *Uncle Tom's Cabin*, which he recommended in March 2002 to high-level state managers for the light it sheds on U.S. history: "Isn't this the government that massacred the original native inhabitants of the land of America? That wiped out the American Indians? Wasn't it this system and its agents who seized millions of Africans from their houses and carried them off into slavery and kidnapped their young sons and daughters to become slaves and inflicted on them for long years the most severe tragedies? Today, one of the most tragic works of art is *Uncle Tom's Cabin*. . . . This book still lives after almost 200 years."

THE BUDDING ISLAMIST

Yet if Khamenei frequented prerevolutionary secular intellectual circles and was a student of Western culture more generally, he was first and foremost a seminarian, devoted to pursuing social change in accordance with the teachings of religion. And in this regard, it was Qutb, the Egyptian intellectual, activist, and chief theoretician of the Muslim Brotherhood, who stole Khamenei's heart as a young man.

Qutb, who was executed by Egyptian President Gamal Abdel Nasser's regime in 1966, propagated the idea of an Islamic state. As he wrote in *The Battle Between Islam and Capitalism*,

> If you want Islam to be an agent of salvation, you must rule and must understand that this religion has not come for one to sit in houses of worship; it hasn't come to make a nest in hearts. Rather, it has come to govern and run life in a proper fashion; it has come to build a progressive and complete society. . . . If we want Islam to answer social, ethnic, and other problems and solve our problems and show a way to cure them, we must think about government and its formation and bring our decisions to implementation. . . . Islam without government and a Muslim nation without Islam are meaningless.

The pillars of Qutb's idea of Islamic government were justice, equality, and the redistribution of wealth. "True Islam," he wrote in *Social Justice in Islam*, "is a liberation movement that frees the hearts of individuals and then of human societies from fear of the bonds of the powerful."

Qutb's ideas would go on to become the template for the modern Salafi movement, eventually influencing radical Islamists such as Osama bin Laden and Ayman al-Zawahiri. They were also very appealing for Iranian seminary students. Khamenei read them, was attracted to Qutb's personality and to some of his ideas, and went so far as to translate some of the master's works into Persian himself. As Khamenei wrote in the introduction to his 1967 translation of Qutb's *The Future of This Religion*, "This lofty and great author has tried in the course of the chapters of this book . . . to first introduce the essence of the faith as it is and then, after showing that it is a program for living . . . [confirm] with his eloquent words and his particular world outlook that ultimately world government shall be in the hands of our school and 'the future belongs to Islam.'"

Qutb revived the classic Muslim concepts of the House of Islam and the House of War but gave them a new meaning: "There is only one House of Islam, and that is precisely the one in which an Islamic state has been founded, and God's sharia rules, and the divine punishments are applied, and in which Muslims support each other. Aside from this, everything is the House of War, and the relationship of the Muslim with it is either war or peace based on a treaty with it."

Qutb also offered Khamenei a perspective on the United States as something of a licentious society, ideas Qutb had picked up during his sojourn there in the late 1940s. Qutb came to feel that Americans were prepared to accept Islam, but not in its true, non-subservient incarnation:

> These days, the Americans have come to think about Islam once more. They need Islam to fight against communism in the Middle East and the Islamic countries of Asia and Africa. . . . Of course, the Islam that America and the Western imperialists and their allies in the Middle East want is not the same Islam that fights imperialism and struggles against absolutism; rather, it is that Islam that struggles against the Communists. Thus, they do not want the Islam that rules and definitely do not want an Islamic government, since when Islam rules, it sets up another *ummah* [Islamic community] and teaches the nations that it is obligatory to become strong, and that rejecting imperialism is a necessity, and that the Communists, too, are like the imperialist pests, and that both are enemies and aggressive.

AFTER THE REVOLUTION

In the early days of the Iranian Revolution, after Washington announced that it was letting the ailing shah into the United States for medical treatment, a group of radical Iranian students seized the U.S. embassy in Tehran and held its occupants hostage, creating a new crisis in U.S.-Iranian relations. Not all the members of the new ruling elite had known about the plan or agreed with it. According to former Iranian President Ali Akbar Hashemi Rafsanjani, neither he nor Khamenei supported the move:

> Ayatollah Khamenei and I were in Mecca when we heard news of the seizure of the American embassy over the radio at night, when we were on the roof of our domicile preparing to sleep. We were shocked, since we had no expectation of such an event. It was not our politics. Even early into the revolution's victory, when political groups shouted very extreme anti-American slogans, the officials helped Americans who were in Iran return to their country uninjured, and many of them even carried their property with them. Once, when an armed group attacked the American embassy and occupied it, a representative came on behalf of the provisional government and settled the problem. Thus, it is clear that neither the revolutionary council nor the provisional government was inclined to take such measures.

But after Khomeini came out in support of the embassy takeover, the other rulers of the Islamic Republic followed his lead. As Khamenei put it in April 1999,

> I, along with Mr. Hashemi and another individual, met with Imam [Khomeini] after traveling from Tehran to Qom to ask, "What are we finally going to do with these spies?" Should they remain, or should we not keep them, particularly since there was an amazing tumult in the provisional government over what we were to do with them? When we came into the imam's presence and our friends explained the situation and said what the [foreign] radio stations were saying, what America was saying, what government officials were saying, he thought and then answered in the form of a question· "Are you afraid of America?" We said, "No." He said, "Then keep them."

During his tenure as supreme leader, Khamenei has always defended the seizure. Revolutionary regimes often maintain their relationships with former colonial powers and suffer as a result, he argues. In the Iranian case, the embassy takeover helped make that impossible: "The matter of the den of spies [the revolutionaries' term for the U.S. embassy] cut the last possible thread connecting the revolution and America," he noted in a speech in 1993. The embassy takeover, he said, "was a great and valuable service performed for our revolution."

Khomeini appointed Khamenei as a member of the Council of the Islamic Revolution, and before becoming president of the republic in 1981, he served as deputy defense minister, acting chair of the Islamic Revolutionary Guard Corps, and Khomeini's representative in the Supreme Defense Council. His work on security issues brought him face-to-face with Washington's cold realpolitik. In August 1980, Saddam Hussein launched a military attack on Iran, trying to take advantage of the new regime's disarray. Still stinging from the fall of the shah and the ongoing hostage crisis, the United States refused to criticize Iraq's actions, first protecting Iraq from censure at the United Nations and then actually supporting the Iraqi war effort against Iran. By the late 1980s, the U.S. military was increasingly engaging Iran directly, including attacking Iranian oil rigs in the Persian Gulf in 1987 and shooting down an Iranian passenger plane in 1988.

In 1987, Khamenei took his only trip to date to the United States, in order to participate as Iran's president in a session of the UN General Assembly. In his speech, he addressed the relationship between Iran and the United States:

> The history of our nation is in a black, bitter, and bloody chapter, mixed with varieties of hostility and spite from the American regime. [That regime] is culpable in 25 years of support of the Pahlavi dictatorship, with all the crimes it committed against our people. The looting of this nation's wealth with the shah's help, the intense confrontation with the revolution during the last months of the shah's regime, its encouragement in crushing the demonstrations of millions of people, its sabotage of the revolution through various means in the first years of its victory, the American embassy in Tehran's provocative contacts with counterrevolutionary elements, the aid to coup plotters and terrorist and counterrevolutionary elements outside the country, the blockading of Iranian cash and property and refusal to transfer goods whose payment had long been received or assets that the shah

had taken from the national wealth and deposited in his own name in American banks, the striving to enforce an economic embargo and the creation of a united Western front against our nation, the open and effective support of Iraq in its war against us, and, finally, an irrational, thuggish invasion of the Persian Gulf that seriously threatened the region's security and tranquility—all this is only part of our nation's indictment against the regime in the United States of America.

In a public speech the following year, he related an experience he'd had while staying in New York: "A high-ranking official of a European country came to meet me and said, 'You should finally solve your problem with America!' They thought that [with my] having come to New York and being in America, they might be able to warm their bread in this oven. I said, 'Impossible. The issue of the UN is another story. I have come to the UN to speak with the people of the world, and this has nothing to do with America. The issue of America is another story.'"

FROM KHOMEINI TO KHAMENEI

Since becoming supreme leader in 1989, Khamenei has sharpened his views of U.S. policy. His position now is clear and simple: Western governments, led by Washington, wish to overthrow the Islamic Republic and destroy the Islamic revolution, just as they did to the Soviet Union.

At a meeting with Iranian government officials in 2000, he put it this way: "An all-encompassing American plan has been arranged to collapse the Islamic Republican system, and all its aspects have been weighed. This plan is reconstructed from the collapse of the Soviet Union. . . . They have, in their own imaginings, revived the plan for the collapse of the Soviets in accordance with the conditions in Iran." Khamenei noted that there had been domestic factors responsible for the Soviet Union's collapse, including poverty, repression, corruption, and ethnic and nationalist tensions. But the Americans capitalized on these, he argued, to push the Soviet state to collapse—partly by manipulating the media and staging a "cultural invasion," and partly by using political and economic pressure. However, such efforts would not work in Iran, he argued, because the Islamic Republic was not like the Soviet Union—not least because, unlike communism, Islam was not a newly adopted ideology imposed by a ruling party after winning a civil war. Iran, moreover, had a long history of unified statehood. Its constituent elements had not been yoked together through imperialist expansion and wars of conquest over recent centuries, as was the case with the Russian empire that the Soviet system inherited. He also noted that the Islamic Republic was the product of a popular revolution and enjoyed considerable religious legitimacy.

Khamenei thinks several measures can ensure that the Islamic Republic does not meet the Soviet Union's fate. First, potential political insurgents—the local Iranian versions of Boris Yeltsin—must be identified and checked. Second, sensible reforms must be announced clearly, so they cannot be misunderstood or perverted. Reform measures must, as he has described, "be led by a powerful and restraining center so that they don't get out of control." Third, the media must not be allowed to undermine the government. And fourth, interference by outside powers, such as the United States and Israel, must be kept at bay.

Khamenei also thinks that the United States, the West more generally, and Israel want to use elections to various Iranian offices (city councils, the legislature, the judiciary, the Assembly of Experts) to create, through their "internal allies," a situation of "dual sovereignty." The aim is, according to Khamenei, to create a split between the supreme leader and elected officials of the government. Just as the British, who once had absolute rulers, eventually turned the position of their monarch into a merely ceremonial office, so Iran's enemies, Khamenei believes, want to turn the absolute rule of the *faqih*, or "guardianship of the jurist," into a meaningless shell. Iran's chief reformist strategist, Saeed Hajjarian, used the concept of dual sovereignty as an analytic tool to describe the changing balance of power in Iran following the victory of Mohammad Khatami in the May 1997 presidential election. In response, Khamenei loyalists tried to assassinate Hajjarian in March 1999. He survived, but he has been paralyzed ever since. Khamenei mentioned the concept of dual sovereignty as a subversive idea in a public speech in 2004, as the Khatami administration limped through its final year in office: "You have heard the slogan 'dual sovereignty'! A number of irrational people have even repeated these words within the country. . . . Dual sovereignty is not desirable but damaging and a deadly poison! This is what [Iran's enemies] want."

After Iran's presidential election in June 2009, hundreds of thousands of people poured out into the streets of Tehran and held peaceful demonstrations against the manipulated outcome. As the demonstrations spread, Khamenei, in a Friday prayer speech, compared the protests to the "color revolutions," particularly the one in Georgia, which he claimed the Americans and the British had launched. Khamenei emphasized that during the previous weeks, the speeches of American and European statesmen had become harsher, and that after the Tehran protests, they set aside their "masks" and showed their "true features."

In a public speech in June 2011, Khamenei called the protests, which came to be known as the Green Movement, a continuation of the regime-change policy of United States and its allies and contrasted it with a true revolution, such as the one that led to the founding of the Islamic Republic: "A revolution that cannot defend itself in an age of sedition, against various political or military coup attempts and other such acts, is not alive. This revolution is alive, for it defends itself and indeed prevails and wins. This is certain, as you saw happen [following the protests] in 2009."

A frequent Khamenei theme is the constant presence of foreign threats to the Islamic Republic and the regime's ability to withstand them. The United States and the Western bloc, he argues, want to overthrow the system in Iran and have launched a variety of attempts to do so, including Iraq's military invasion in 1980, the manipulation of ethnic tensions, and economic sanctions. As he put it in another public speech in August 2010,

> They want to bring the revolution down. One of the important means they have employed has been these economic sanctions. They say that [the sanctions] are not targeting the Iranian people, but they are lying! The sanctions are meant to cripple the Iranian nation. They are designed to exhaust the Iranian people and make them say, "We are under the pressure of the sanctions because of the [policies of] the Islamic Republican state." They want to sever the ties between the people and the Islamic Republican system. This is the true aim of the sanctions. They are exerting economic pressure by means of sanctions.

He repeatedly claims that the stated rationales for U.S. policies are meant to mask more sinister motives. As he put it in yet another public speech in August 2011, "Although the excuse for the sanctions is the issue of nuclear energy, they are lying. . . . Perhaps you recall that the first sanctions against this country were enacted at a time when the nuclear issue absolutely did not exist. . . . Thus, the enemy's goal is to hurl the Islamic Republic to the ground."

Khamenei bases such arguments partly on what he sees as two failed attempts by Iran to compromise with the United States. The first was during Khatami's term as president, when the government suspended its uranium enrichment for two years as a trust-building measure. Khamenei believes the Western governments were not interested in trust building, only in making the pause in enrichment permanent. The two-year suspension resulted in no achievements for Iran—not the lifting of sanctions, nor the release of frozen Iranian assets in the United States, nor any other reward. In a speech in January 2008, Khamenei noted,

> Today, to whomever comes to us and says, "Sir, suspend temporarily," we say, "We have already had a temporary suspension, for two years!" We had a two-year temporary suspension. How did it benefit us? . . . We, for our part, imagined that it was temporary and imagined that it was voluntary. Then, when we talked of resuming work, they started this media frenzy and tumult in political circles, saying, "Woe! Iran wants to end

the suspension!" The suspension became a sacred issue that Iran had absolutely no right to approach. . . . Finally, they said, "This temporary suspension isn't enough; you must completely pack the whole atomic project in." This was a setback for us. [The Khatami government] accepted the retreat. But this retreat had a positive effect for us. We learned a lesson from that experience. World public opinion learned from the experience, too. . . . I said if this process of adding new demands is to go on, I will intervene. And I did. I said . . . we should go on the offensive [and resume enrichment].

Khamenei then went on to remind his audience that despite Khatami's willingness to compromise, his kind words for Americans, his cooperation in toppling the Taliban and in the subsequent Bonn negotiations to install a pro-American government in Afghanistan, U.S. President George W. Bush had still included Iran in his "axis of evil."

The second experience he draws on is Libya's 2003 decision to give up its nuclear ambitions, which nevertheless did not prevent Muammar al-Qaddafi's violent removal through NATO military involvement. "In Libya," Khamenei said in his annual Iranian New Year speech in March 2011, "although Qaddafi had shown an anti-Western tendency during his first years in power, in later years, he performed a great service to the West. . . . This gentleman gathered up his nuclear program, . . . gave it to the Westerners, and said, 'Take it away!' . . . [Yet he was overthrown.]" Khamenei suspects that even if all of Iran's nuclear facilities were closed down, or opened up to inspections and monitoring, Western governments would simply pocket the concessions and raise other issues—such as terrorism, human rights, or Israel—as excuses for maintaining their pressure and pursuing regime change. To Khamenei, when it comes to nuclear weapons, the Iraqi and Libyan cases teach the same lesson. Saddam and Qaddafi opened their facilities up to inspections by the West, ended up having no nuclear weapons, and were eventually attacked, deposed, and killed. Major compromises by Iran on the nuclear front without significant concessions by the

West, he believes, could end up leading to similar consequences for the Iranian regime.

SANCTITIES

Another important issue for Khamenei is what he sees as actions that amount to insults to Islam. After the announcement of a possible burning of the Koran by a pastor in Florida in 2010, he asked in one of his public speeches, "What and who is behind the scenes of these evil deeds?" He went on to say that "a careful study of this evil occurrence, which came along with criminal deeds in Afghanistan, Iraq, Palestine, Lebanon, and Pakistan, leaves no doubt that the planning and the operational command of these acts are in the hands of the system of hegemony and Zionist planning centers, which enjoy the greatest influence over the American government and its security and military agencies, as well as the British and some European governments." Similarly, after the release of the film *Innocence of Muslims* in 2012, he published a statement citing the American and Israeli governments as "prime suspects for this crime." He said that "if they had not supported the previous links in this rotten chain—that is, Salman Rushdie, the Danish cartoonist, the American Koran-burning pastor—and did not order dozens of anti-Islamic films from the cliques linked with Zionist capitalists, things would not have reached the point of this great and unforgivable crime."

At the same time, he tries hard to avoid casting this issue as a conflict between Islam and Christianity. "The goal of these infuriating measures [Koran burnings]," he argued in a public speech in September 2010, "is to bring the confrontation with Islam and Muslims into the mainstream of Christian societies and to give it a religious coloration and zeal." But "we must all realize," he said, that this "has nothing to do with churches or Christianity, and the puppet deeds of a few idiotic and mercenary clerics must not be laid at the feet of Christians and their clergy. We Muslims will never commit similar acts in regard to the sanctities of other religions. The struggle between Muslims and Christians on a general level is what the enemies and plotters of these insane displays want, and the Koran instructs us to take the opposite position."

THE DECLINE OF THE WEST

Khamenei does not deny the astonishing progress of the West over the past century. As he said in a public speech in June 2004, "In America, you see the pinnacle of the rise of materialist civilization from the perspective of science, wealth, military power, and political and diplomatic efforts. America is a country that has legendary wealth and military power and extraordinary political mobility." He accepts Western science and technology and laments the fact that despotic regimes in Iran and elsewhere in the developing world are responsible for these countries' underdevelopment. Khamenei admires certain aspects of Western societies. Meeting with youth and cultural affairs workers in the Caspian city of Rasht in 2001, for example, he noted that "one good quality in European people is their willingness to take risks. This is the chief source of their successes. . . . Another of their good qualities is perseverance and keeping at hard work. . . . The greatest and most talented Western inventors and scholars are those who for long years live a hard life sitting in a garret and discover something. When one reads their biographies, one sees what a hard life they lived. . . . These are the good parts of Western culture."

"Western culture," he noted in a discussion with Iranian youths in February 1999, on the occasion of the anniversary of the revolution, "is a combination of beautiful and ugly things. No one can say that Western culture is completely ugly. No, like any other culture, it surely has beautiful manifestations. . . . A sensible nation and a group of sensible people will take the good and add it to their own culture, thus enriching it, and reject the bad." He believes that Islamic civilization is superior, however, because Western civilization is overly materialistic. "The West looks at only one dimension, one feature—the material feature," he said during a recent meeting with youths devoted to the topic of socioeconomic development. He added that the Western outlook considers "progress first and foremost, composed of progress in wealth, science, military affairs, and technology. . . . But in Islamic logic, progress has other dimensions: progress in science, in justice, in public welfare, in economics, in international grandeur and status, in political independence, in prayer and approaching the exalted God—in other words, it has a spiritual aspect, a divine aspect."

Khamenei is not a fan of liberal democracy. He argues that its supposed majoritarian legitimacy is undermined by the fact that actual governments in the West have received the votes of only a small fraction of the total possible electorate. He claims, moreover, that liberal democracies, such as the United States, have repeatedly violated their own principles by supporting despotic governments elsewhere, and have even worked to overthrow democratic regimes (such as with the 1953 coup in Iran). He sees liberal democratic governments as being interested in ruling the world at large, pushing globalization as a route toward Americanization, and attacking other countries at will (such as Afghanistan and Iraq).

The Islamic Republic has its own form of democracy, Khamenei believes, one that is rooted in religion. "The foundations of religious democracy are different from those of Western democracy," he argued in June 2005 in a speech on the anniversary of Khomeini's death. "Religious democracy, which is the basis we have voted for and which arises from the divine rights and duties of man, is not just a contract. All humans have the right to vote and the right to self-determination. This is what lends meaning to elections in the Islamic Republic. [What we have here] is much more advanced and meaningful and deeply rooted than what exists today in Western liberal democracy."

In practice, Khamenei believes that liberal democracy yields not freedom but domination, aggression, and imperialism, and this is what makes it unacceptable. "We believe in democracy," he said in a meeting with members of the Basij militia in northwestern Iran in October 2011. "We believe in freedom, too. But we do not accept liberal democracy. . . . We don't want to use that name for our pure, sound, righteous, and clean meaning. We say Islamic democracy, or the Islamic Republic." For all his criticisms of liberalism, however, he has not prevented the translation into Persian and the publication during his term of the works of liberal authors, such as Karl Popper, Milton Friedman, Ronald Dworkin, Isaiah Berlin, John Rawls, Richard Rorty, Martha Nussbaum, Robert Putnam, Amartya Sen, and many others.

Khamenei believes that Western governments and capitalism in general are suffering from incurable structural problems and face inevitable decline. In June 1992, in a message to pilgrims to Mecca, he said,

The Western capitalist system is sunk to its neck in human problems. Despite the copious wealth that it has at its disposal, it is completely incapable of establishing social justice. The recent riots of blacks in America showed that the American system treats not only the nations of Asia, Africa, and Latin America with injustice but also its own people, and answers protest with violence and repression just like in those other countries. It is true that the communist camp collapsed and vanished, but its rival, the capitalist camp, . . . particularly plagued by the arrogance that has affected it after the disappearance of its powerful rival, will vanish too, sooner or later.

He has argued that the financial crisis that began in 2008 is evidence in support of his pessimistic view of the West's prospects. He saw the Occupy Wall Street protests as the beginning of a major crisis in capitalism. "The people in these meetings and demonstrations of several thousand in New York," he noted at a large gathering of people in the city of Kermanshah in October 2011, "put up a poster on which it was written, 'We are the 99 percent.' In other words, 99 percent of the American people—the majority of the American people—are ruled by a dominant one percent. . . . Today, the capitalist system has reached a complete dead end. Perhaps it will take years for the consequences of this dead end to reach their final conclusion. But the crisis of the West has begun in earnest."

For Khamenei, world history is "turning a corner," and "a new age in the entire world" is beginning. The Marxist, liberal, and nationalist creeds have lost their attraction, and only Islam has kept its. The Arab Spring—or, as he calls it, "the Islamic Awakening"—is a prelude to a worldwide uprising against the United States and international Zionism. In his view, the fact that routine materialistic calculations make such an outcome unlikely is unimportant, because divine providence will bring it about. He sees the survival of the Islamic Republic in the face of more than three decades of international opposition as evidence of this heavenly support and counts on it continuing in the future. Khamenei believes that the historic turn he anticipates will lead to the victory of spiritual and divine values in the world. Contrary to Max Weber's diagnosis that modern science has disenchanted the world and the realm of power, Khamenei still relies on esoteric notions and divine beings in his approach to politics. He is re-enchanting the world.

TALKING ABOUT TALKS

In August 1989, two months after being elected supreme leader, Khamenei announced to the United States,

> No one in the Islamic Republic has ever negotiated with you, nor will they. . . . As long as American policy is based on lies, deception, and duplicity and supports corrupt regimes, like that of Israel, and perpetuates oppression against the weak and poor nations, and as long as crimes and transgressions of the American rulers, such as the downing of the passenger plane and the impounding of Iran's property, remain in our nation's memory, there is no possibility of our holding negotiations with the American government or establishing diplomatic relations with it. We completely reject relations between them and us.

The following year, in a meeting with a group of students on the anniversary of the embassy takeover, he elaborated his thinking on this front:

Those who think that we must negotiate with . . . America are either simple-minded or frightened. . . . What would negotiations mean? Would all problems be solved if only you go and sit with America and talk and negotiate? This is not the case. Negotiations with America mean trading with America. Trade means you get something and you give something. What will you give to America from the Islamic revolution for which you will get something? . . . Do you know what it wants? By God, America is not upset with the Iranian nation for anything more than its being Muslim, its standing firm with Muhammad's pure Islam. It wants you to stop being so firm. It wants you to not be proud. Are you ready for that?

Seventeen years later, in December 2007, at a gathering of students in the central city of Yazd, he returned to the topic:

One of our fundamental policies is cutting relations with America. Yet we have never said that we will cut these relations forever. No, there is no reason to cut relations forever with any state. . . . [But] relations with America are harmful to us. First, establishing relations will not reduce the danger posed by America. America attacked Iraq while the countries had diplomatic relations. . . . Second, having relations with the Americans is a way for them to increase their influence within certain strata . . . in Iran. . . . They need a base that they don't have now. This is what they want. They want their intelligence officers to be able to travel to Iran without restrictions. . . . Some people brag about the harm that results from the absence of [diplomatic] relations. No, gentlemen! Not having relations with America is good for us. The day when relations with America will be beneficial, I will be the first one to say that relations should be established.

In August 2010, in a meeting with high-level officials of the government under President Mahmoud Ahmadinejad, Khamenei offered his interpretation of "two recent cases of negotiations with the United States, one of which was related to problems in Iraq." This was at a time when Ahmadinejad had stated that he was ready to negotiate with the United States. Khamenei described his understanding of the U.S. negotiating style:

When the Americans don't have strong arguments, when they cannot present an argument that is acceptable and logical, they resort to bullying. And since bullying has no effect on the Islamic Republic, they unilaterally declare the end of negotiations! Fine, what kind of negotiation is that? This is our experience in both cases. So, when people like Mr. President [Ahmadinejad] say that we are ready to negotiate, I say yes, we are ready to negotiate, but not with the United States. The reason is that America does not enter the field honestly, like an ordinary negotiator; it enters into negotiations like a super-power. . . . Let them set aside threats, let them set aside sanctions, let them not insist that the negotiations must end in a specific conclusion. [Then there can be negotiations.]

In February 2013, attending a security conference in Munich, U.S. Vice President Joseph Biden said that in its efforts to prevent Iran from acquiring nuclear weapons, the United States had imposed "the most robust sanctions in history" and that Iran's leaders were punishing their own people through economic deprivation and international isolation. Biden indicated that diplomacy still had a chance but that direct talks would be possible only "when the Iranian leadership, the supreme leader, is serious."

Khamenei responded quickly and directly. In a speech to the commanders of the Iranian air force, he said that since U.S. President Barack Obama's election in 2008, he had announced that the Iranian leadership would take an unprejudiced look at the new government's behavior and then make a decision. But what had been the results of Obama's first term? Washington had supported the "internal rebellion" (the Green Movement); it had imposed crippling sanctions that, he claimed, U.S. Secretary of State Hillary Clinton said were intended to foment a popular uprising against the Islamic Republic; it had turned a blind eye to Israel's assassinations of Iran's nuclear scientists and perhaps even backed them; and it had supported the same terrorists in Syria that they had overthrown in Afghanistan in 2001. He then addressed Biden's call for talks:

Whom did you want to cripple [with sanctions]? Did you want to paralyze the Iranian people? Is there any goodwill in this? . . . I am not a diplomat. I am a revolutionary and talk in a clear and forthright manner. . . .

> Diplomats say something, and they mean something else. We talk
> in honest and clear terms. . . . Negotiations are meaningful when the
> other side shows its goodwill. When the other side does not show any
> goodwill, when you yourselves say pressure and negotiations, these
> two don't go together. You want to point a gun at the Iranian people
> and say, "Negotiate, or I'll fire." . . . You should know that the Iranian
> people will not be frightened as a result of such acts.

Khamenei claimed that the Islamic Republic was ready for direct negotiations with Washington but that there were several necessary preconditions. He wants the United States to give up what
he sees as its attempts to overthrow the Islamic Republic, enter
into negotiations in a spirit of mutual respect and equality, and
abandon its simultaneous efforts to pressure Iran, such as with military threats and economic sanctions. He argues that on these matters, contrary to what Biden said in Munich, the ball is in Washington's court, not Tehran's.

Khamenei rejects the notion that the differences between Iran
and the United States center on the nuclear program. "If we wanted
to make nuclear weapons," he said in a public meeting with a del-
egation of ulama and martyrs' families from the Iranian region of
Azerbaijan this past February,

> how could you prevent it? If Iran was determined to have nuclear
> weapons, America could not prevent it in any way. We do not want to
> make nuclear weapons. Not because America is upset over this, but
> because it's our own belief. We believe that nuclear weapons are a
> crime against humanity and must not be produced and that those that
> already exist in the world must be eliminated. This is our belief. It has
> nothing to do with you. If we did not have this belief and decided to
> make nuclear weapons, no power could prevent us, just as they were
> not able to prevent it in other places—not in India, not in Pakistan,
> not in North Korea.

The key to successful negotiations, he claims, is for Washington
to change its attitude and sense of entitlement. "The Americans
must confirm their good intentions and show that they are not interested in bullying. If they demonstrate this, then they will see

that the Iranian nation will respond in kind. Let them not make trouble, let them not intervene, let them not bully, let them recognize the Iranian nation's rights. Then they will receive a commensurate response from Iran."

Every year, Khamenei gives his most important speech in Mashhad on the first day of spring, the beginning of the Iranian New Year. This year's address was striking, however, for what seemed to be a slight softening of his position on talks. For the first time, even while expressing his lack of optimism about direct negotiations with the United States, he explicitly said, "But I don't oppose them." And while noting that Washington seems to have no inclination to complete the nuclear negotiations and resolve the issue, he nevertheless said that the solution to the conflict "is very near and very simple." Iran's only demand, he said, was recognition of its right to enrich uranium for peaceful purposes, and it would be "very simple" to eliminate foreigners' concerns. "They can implement the nuclear agency's legal regulations; from the start, we, for our part, have had no opposition to implementing these supervisions and regulations."

What is noteworthy about the road traveled by the supreme leader during these tumultuous past three decades is the change in the manner of his discourse. He has shifted away from absolute ideological notions of "the West," "world arrogance," and the United States as a totally homogenous other and moved toward accepting a more nuanced conception of the West as a complex social reality—one with not only an inherent drive to ruthless market competition, capitalist exploitation and foreign policy expansion but also dynamic artistic products, literature, science and technology, risk taking and institutional innovations, and religious and spiritual diversity. The discourse depicting the United States as an absolute enemy with which it would be absurd and naive even to think about negotiating has given way to a discourse about the United States as a potential interlocutor with which it might be possible to discuss acceptable terms of negotiations over such issues as the nuclear program and security in Iraq. It appears that for Khamenei, the United States has gone from being the monstrous absolute other to a powerful regional presence with a domestic political system plagued by the painful consequences of two recent failed military adventures in the Middle East.

WHAT COMES NEXT?

Given Khamenei's control over Iranian policy and his deeply rooted suspicion of U.S. intentions toward the Islamic Republic, improving the relationship between Iran and the United States will be difficult, especially if long-standing U.S. policies, such as constantly escalating sanctions, remain in place. Yet improved relations are not impossible, because the most important interests of both Tehran and Washington can indeed be accommodated simultaneously.

What Khamenei needs to know is that Washington is not determined to cripple or overthrow the Islamic Republic, and what the United States needs to know is that the Iranian nuclear project is peaceful, that Iran will not block free access to energy resources and regional sea-lanes, and that Israel can enjoy peace and security within its internationally recognized borders (which, some still hope, will be determined in a final settlement with the Palestinians). Iran can reassure Western governments that its nuclear project is peaceful by making it transparent and by ratifying and implementing the International Atomic Energy Agency's Additional Protocols on proliferation safeguards in exchange for its guaranteed right under the Nuclear Nonproliferation Treaty to enrich uranium for peaceful purposes. The West, in turn, can reassure Iran that it is not bent on regime change by taking tangible practical measures in exchange for Iranian adherence to security and peace in the Persian Gulf and the wider Middle East—and it will have to do so in order to make significant progress on the nuclear front.

Washington would be well advised to lift the economic sanctions, since whatever their aims, sanctions inflict damage on populations at large, not only or even primarily on the government officials who are their ostensible targets. This is as true in Iran as it is elsewhere, and it means that outside powers, and the United States in particular, are currently responsible for widespread unemployment, soaring inflation, and a massive increase in poverty. Under these circumstances, more and more middle-class families will join the ranks of the poor, and more children of the poor will fall victim to malnutrition, disease, and violence. Problems of daily survival will become the public's main concern, issues of democracy and human rights will be marginalized, and Iran's social fabric will be destroyed from within—just as happened in Iraq during the 1990s. That is not something the United States should want to see for any number of reasons.

Khamenei, for his part, must accept that in the long run, the only way to make the Islamic Republic truly powerful and sustainable is to legitimize his regime through the people's free votes. The Soviet Union had the largest army in the world and amassed thousands of nuclear weapons, but it eventually collapsed. Even if Western governments forswear any intentions of regime change, Iran's domestic problems will never be solved without democracy, freedom, and human rights.

If the Obama administration is serious about pursuing a solution to the problems between Tehran and Washington, it would be well advised to develop a road map that specifies the unresolved issues in the Iranian nuclear file in a clear manner and sets out a timeline for investigating, resolving, and closing the cases one by one. Step-by-step progress on the nuclear front should be linked to step-by-step progress on lifting the sanctions. The administration would also be well advised to take a comprehensive approach to the region and embed discussions of the Iranian nuclear program in a broader framework of regional security, bringing Washington's allies on board and minimizing those allies' desire to play the spoiler. This would mean building a consensus around a set of rules for regional politics, guaranteeing borders and abjuring regime change as a policy, achieving real results in ending the impasse in the Israeli-Palestinian peace process, working toward the eventual removal of weapons of mass destruction from the region, and supporting human rights across the Middle East.

This is obviously a very tall order, but there is no other way to avoid the continuation, or even escalation, of the existing conflicts in the region. Confrontational policies on all sides over the last decade have yielded little except stalemate and misery. The election of Rouhani as president showed the desire of the Iranian people to put a decisive end to the Ahmadinejad era, and it has created an opportunity for both Iran and the international community to move forward toward more constructive relations. That opportunity should be seized rather than ignored.🌐

Why Rouhani Won— And Why Khamenei Let Him

The Ahmadinejad Era Comes to an Auspicious End

Suzanne Maloney

Four years ago, after the dubious reelection of Iranian President Mahmoud Ahmadinejad, the Iranian streets were filled with protestors demanding to know what had happened to their votes. This weekend, the voters finally got their answer—and, once more, they filled the country's streets. This time, though, they were celebrating as the government confirmed that Hassan Rouhani, the presidential candidate who had campaigned on promises of reform and reopening to the world, had won an overwhelming victory.

The election of Rouhani, a centrist cleric who has been close to Iran's apex of power since the 1979 revolution, is an improbably auspicious end to the Ahmadinejad era. Rouhani is a blunt pragmatist with plenty of experience maneuvering within Iran's theocratic system. He is far too sensible to indulge in a power grab à la Ahmadinejad. And, as a cleric, he assuages the fears of the Islamic Republic's religious class. He embraced reformist rhetoric during the campaign, but will not deviate too far from the system's

SUZANNE MALONEY is a Senior Fellow at the Saban Center for Middle East Policy at the Brookings Institution.

principles, the foremost of which is the primacy of the Supreme Leader. Meanwhile, Rouhani's focus on the economic costs of Ahmadinejad's mismanagement resonates with the regime's traditionalists as well as with a population battered by a decade of intensifying hardship and repression. All in all, the new president might benefit from a broader base of support than any in Iran's post-revolutionary history, which will be an important asset as he seeks to navigate the country out of isolation and economic crisis.

Going into the election, a Rouhani victory seemed unlikely. The conservatives' favored candidate was said to be Saeed Jalili, a pious and prim bureaucrat who was appointed as lead nuclear negotiator six years ago. Jalili's chief qualifications for the post were his status as a "living martyr" (he lost a leg in the war with Iraq), his discolored forehead (from dutiful prayer), and his cultivation of Ayatollah Ali Khamenei over the past ten years. It is easy to understand why Jalili was seen as leading the pack; he is basically an improved version of Ahmadinejad, a younger generation hard-liner who boasts total commitment to the ideals of the revolution but who, given his limited national profile, would be perfectly subservient to Khamenei.

By contrast, Rouhani initially drummed up minimal excitement within Iran and even less attention outside the country, despite the implicit imprimatur of Ali Akbar Hashemi Rafsanjani, Iran's foremost power broker. Because the clergy is so unpopular in Iran at the moment, and because the hard-liners disparaged Rouhani's track record on the nuclear issue almost non-stop, his prospects seemed dim. Further, in the unlikely event that his campaign did gain steam, it seemed, hard-liners would have no qualms about doing whatever it took to neutralize a potential threat.

In retrospect, though, it is easy to see that Rouhani had a number of things going for him. First, his campaign was sharper than many gave it credit for. He pushed against the regime's red lines, for example, by promising to release political prisoners. And, in a clear reference to Mir Hossein Mousavi and Mehdi Karroubi, two reformist candidates who were detained after the 2009 vote, he said that he would free all those who remain under house arrest as well. Rouhani sparred heatedly with Jalili's campaign chief and bypassed state media by releasing a compelling video that highlighted his experience during the war with Iraq (he was on the Supreme Defense Council, was a member of the High Council for Supporting War, and was commander of the Iran Air Defense Force, among other roles) and on nuclear negotiations (he was Iran's top nuclear negotiator from 2003 to 2005). His aggressive campaign caught the attention of a disaffected Iranian population, who eventually began to throng his rallies.

Rouhani also benefitted from an unprecedented alliance between Iran's embattled reform movement and the center-right faction to which Rouhani, as well as Rafsanjani, are generally understood to belong. The division between the two factions dates back to the earliest years of the revolution. It became more entrenched after the reformists gained power in 1997, when Mohammad Khatami, the reformist standard-bearer, was elected president in a major upset. By joining with the center-right now, the reformists got a path out of the political desert in which they have languished since the end of Khatami's presidency. By joining with the reformists, Rouhani got a powerful get-out-the-vote effort and the withdrawal from the race of Mohammad Reza Aref, the sole approved reformist candidate. By contrast, the conservative camp remained divided, never coalescing around a single candidate. Had it managed to do so, it could have at least forced the election into a run-off.

Of course, Rouhani's most powerful advantage was the bitter unhappiness of the Iranian people, who have witnessed the implosion of their currency, the return of austerity measures not seen since the Iran-Iraq War, and the erosion of their basic rights and freedoms over the past eight years. The fact that they were willing to hope again, even after the crushing disappointment of 2009 election, underscores a remarkable commitment to peaceful change and to democratic institutions.

All this might explain the massive turnout on election day and Rouhani's overwhelming popular victory. It does not explain, though, why Khamenei avoided the chicanery that plagued the 2009 vote and why he let the result stand.

One explanation is that the Ayatollah simply miscalculated and found himself, once again, overtaken by events when Rouhani's candidacy surged with little forewarning. Indeed, it is likely that Khamenei really did expect Iranians to vote for the conservatives. After all, the conservatives have held all the cards in Iran since 2005; they dominate its institutions and dictate the terms of the debate. With the leading reformists imprisoned or in exile, no one expected that the forces of change could be revived so powerfully. When his expectations proved off base last Friday, Khamenei could have simply opted not to risk a repeat of 2009.

There is another possibility, however, and one that better explains Khamenei's strangely permissive attitude toward Rouhani's edgy campaign and toward the extraordinary debate that took place between the eight remaining presidential candidates on state television only a week before the election. In that discussion, an exchange about general foreign policy issues morphed unexpectedly into a mutiny on the nuclear issue. One candidate, Ali Akbar Velayati, a scion of the regime's conservative base, attacked Jalili for failing to strike a nuclear deal and for permitting U.S.-backed sanctions on Iran to increase.

The amazingly candid discussion that followed Velayati's charge betrayed the Iranian establishment's awareness of the regime's increasing vulnerability. It could only be understood as an intervention—one initiated by the regime's most stalwart supporters and intended to rescue the system by acknowledging its precarious straits and appealing for pragmatism (rather than Jalili's dogmatism). The discussion was also an acknowledgement that the sanctions-induced miseries of the Iranian public can no longer be soothed with nuclear pageantry or even appeals to religious nationalism.

It is therefore possible to imagine that Khamenei's unexpected munificence, including his last-minute appeal for every Iranian—even those who don't support the Islamic Republic—to vote, was planned. In this case, those who see Rouhani's election as a replay of the shocking political upset that Khatami pulled off in 1997 are off base. Instead, Rouhani's election is an echo of Khamenei's sudden shift in 1988 and 1989, when he charged Rafsanjani, a pragmatist, with ending the war with Iraq, and then helped Rafsanjani win the presidency so that he could spearhead the post-war reconstruction program. Now, as then, Khamenei is not bent on infinite sacrifice. Perhaps allowing Rouhani's victory is his way of empowering a conciliator to repair Iran's frayed relations with the world and find some resolution to the nuclear dispute that enables the country to revive oil exports and resume normal trade.

That does not mean, of course, that Rouhani has an easy road ahead. He must wrangle the support of the hard-liners and lock in at least continued tacit backing from Khamenei. In doing so, he will have to overcome a decade of resentment. During his stint leading nuclear talks, Rouhani made the sole serious concession that the Islamic Republic has ever offered on its nuclear ambitions: a multi-year suspension of its enrichment activities that was ended just before Ahmadinejad took office.

The move won Rouhani the unending fury of the hard-liners, including Khamenei, who approved the deal but has publicly inveighed against Rouhani's nuclear diplomacy as recently as last summer. Today, however, many Iranians—including, apparently, many within the establishment—find his ability to craft a viable deal with the world on the nuclear issue appealing. His election thus suggests that a historic shift in Iran's approach to the world and to the nuclear standoff could be in the offing. Still, to overcome old antipathies among the conservatives and to advance his agenda for change within Iran's Machiavellian political culture, Rouhani will need the clear and unwavering support of Khamenei, something that the Supreme Leader has only accorded to one president during his 25-year tenure: Ahmadinejad, in his first term.

For Washington, meanwhile, the election offered stark confirmation that its strategy is working, at least to a point. The outcome confirmed that political will for a nuclear deal exists within the Islamic Republic. Even with a more moderate president at the helm, however, the nuclear issue will not be readily resolved, and Iran's divided political sphere is as difficult as ever. To overcome the deep-seated (and not entirely unjustified) paranoia of its ultimate decision-maker, the United States will need to be patient. It will need to understand, for example, that Rouhani will need to demonstrate to Iranians that he can produce tangible rewards for diplomatic overtures. That means that Washington should be prepared to offer significant sanctions relief in exchange for any concessions on the nuclear issue. Washington will also have to understand that Rouhani may face real constraints in seeking to solve the nuclear dispute without exacerbating the mistrust of the hardliners. And all the while, the Obama administration will have to proceed cautiously, since appearing too effusive will diminish Rouhani's domestic standing.

In other words, the path out of isolation and economic crisis is perilous, but Iran's new president, who has sometimes been dubbed "the sheikh of diplomacy," may just be the right man at the right moment to walk it.

Rouhani's Gorbachev Moment

What Makes a Genuine Reformer?

Stephen Kotkin

C ould Iranian President Hassan Rouhani be another Mikhail Gorbachev—a real reformer who opens his country's political system and creates the space for détente with the United States and Europe?

Historical analogies are always fraught, of course, and leaders who are championed as reformers almost always leave disillusionment in their wakes. In addition, the jury is still out on whether a nuclear deal between the United States and Iran, which would open the door for a relaxation of painful sanctions, is even a good idea—the specifics of the agreement matter greatly.

But whichever side one comes down on, it is worth considering where the Islamic Republic might be headed. In that regard, there are a few areas to watch.

NOTHING LEFT TO LOSE

Gorbachev was unique, a true believer in Soviet renewal who sat at the very top of a profoundly centralized political system.

Rouhani is nothing like him. In fact, Rouhani came to power precisely because of Tehran's deep fragmentation, particularly within its right-wing establishment. The fracturing created an opening that Rouhani burst through in a surprise electoral victory in June 2013.

STEPHEN KOTKIN is a professor of history and international affairs at Princeton University.

But it also means that he cannot impose far-reaching reform. No one in Iran could, not even Supreme Leader Ayatollah Khamenei. (If anything, the ceaseless invocations of Khamenei's "supreme" authority testify to its absence, as well as his desire to have it.)

That said, the Iran state structure is similar to that of the former Soviet Union in some respects. Namely, both were born of revolution, which created a theocracy—in one case with a clerical establishment, in the other with a Communist party—that overrode the formal institutions of the state, such as parliaments, judiciaries, and civil service. In Iran, as in the Soviet Union in the 1980s, the revolution is aging, with far-reaching consequences. An official ideology, whether Marxism-Leninism or political Islam, can give a regime great power. But it can also destabilize the theocratic system if the populace and the rulers lose faith. And there, Iran is vulnerable.

A second similarity can be found in Iran's imperial overstretch. It is problematic enough that Iran's geopolitical ambitions significantly exceed its capabilities. But it is really taxing that the places and causes in which the country has chosen to become enmeshed are so volatile. Soviet leaders would sympathize: as KGB analysts ruefully lamented, mostly after the collapse of the union, the regime's allies almost always seemed to be impoverished basket cases whose only industry was perpetual civil war. Working with them might have poked the United States in the eye. But it did little for Soviet prestige, economic well-being, and security. From Afghanistan and Angola to Cuba and Yemen, to say nothing of North Korea, hawkish Soviet foreign policy often resembled a very determined stomp on a rake. (Thwack.)

Something similar, on a smaller scale, could be said of Iran's foreign policy. By now, most Americans understand that the intervention in Iraq (the second Iraq War), waged at great cost in American blood and treasure, redounded to Iran's geopolitical benefit. Many analysts argue that the United States' failure to intervene militarily in Syria did the same. But it is difficult to pinpoint, precisely, what Iran gained in Iraq or Syria. It is unclear that Iranian regional "successes" improved its security or its citizens' well-being. One could even argue that Iran's support for mischief (and worse) has only heightened the regime's vulnerability—just like the domestic failures of political Islamism.

Like the Soviet Union, Iran lives in a tough geopolitical neighborhood, one that has only been getting tougher. Statelets concocted by French and British colonial officials, the bankruptcy of pan-Arab nationalism, the recent struggles to the death between hopelessly corrupt authoritarians and the opposition (which is also often authoritarian), some violent de facto partitions—these have created a regional tangle that inflicts immense suffering and that no outside power can readily unknot.

Simply put, U.S. policy in the Middle East is in shambles because the Middle East is in shambles. Iran's Middle East policy is in shambles too. Persistently playing the role of spoiler in one's own neighborhood brings few long-term rewards—and that is even before the recent round of international sanctions (a stunning achievement made possible by the fact that China and Russia, as much as they chafe at U.S. power, dislike any kind of revisionism other than their own). Thanks to Iran's behavior, its neighborhood has become still more treacherous, and the pain is multiplied by the country's international isolation, high inflation, and collapsing currency.

At this point, Iran has little to lose but its own chains if it reforms and cooperates with the West. Of course, that is no guarantee that it will. Just because something is necessary does not mean that it is politically feasible. In fact, Iran's political establishment is far from ready for a drastic turnabout in relations with the Great Satan. The structures that facilitated the U.S.-Iranian alliance during the Cold War are long gone—the genuine Soviet menace, the strongman regime installed by a U.S.-sponsored coup, even the intense dependency on foreign oil. At the same time, the U.S. alliance with Israel, Iran's sworn enemy, has only deepened. Any mini-détente with the United States, which is vital for Iran's domestic development, is going to require far-reaching domestic changes.

And herein lies Rouhani's Gorbachev moment.

CONDITIONALITY

Gorbachev was able to push through deep reform for three reasons. First, everything he did was in the name of renewing the system. Second, he was a master political tactician, at least within the context of the Soviet Communist system, and had promoted hapless conservatives to key positions at the head of the central Communist Party secretariat, the Soviet military, and the KGB. Third, U.S. President Ronald Reagan not only put major pressure on the Soviets but, when the concessions came, showed the foresight—and had the credibility—to pocket them and afford Gorbachev a lot of running room domestically.

It is hard to imagine Rouhani meeting all three of these conditions. Were he to introduce major domestic reforms, including an end to clerical disqualification of electoral candidates and to Basij and Revolutionary Guard control over large swaths of the economy, he would certainly claim that they are in the name of renewing the system. And he did show some Gorbachev-esque skill when he seized on a political moment, won elections, and promptly hinted at the possibility for nuclear negotiations. Further, he is already working overtime to further divide and conquer the hard-liners. But it is less certain that he will find a deft negotiator in Washington—one able to cut a deal and keep to it, and to deepen that deal over time should Iran begin to institute major reforms.

And that is not all. An even greater challenge for Rouhani will be to find a path toward reform that does not also destabilize the regime. Parsing the news out of Tehran, it is hard to say what the regime's plan is. In fact, beyond winning sanctions relief and ending isolation, Rouhani might not have one. The Iranian public, media, and academic institutions, as well as the diaspora, seem to have plenty of bold ideas. But as Gorbachev found, it is not enough to be bold. There has to be a tenable end state—a safer and better place—into which the system can settle. If there isn't, Rouhani could indeed turn out to be Gorbachev: a man who is not able to reform his polity without unintentionally liquidating it.

1989 AND 2013

The final question, then, is how observers can judge whether any apparent reforms are for real. This was one of the great problems with deciphering Gorbachev too. Analysts could not tell what was going on because Gorbachev effectively claimed to be both undertaking radical change and not undertaking radical change at all. He was democratizing the Communist Party, revitalizing the Soviets with elections, energizing central planning with some decentralization and market mechanisms, and pursuing peace abroad. Skeptics had an easy time dismissing these initiatives, which sounded very Communist, very Soviet.

Gorbachev did not come out and say, "I am going to end the Communist Party monopoly," because that was never his intention. It was only a consequence of allowing alternative civic associations to form, relaxing censorship, and introducing competitive elections. He never said, "I am going to destroy economic planning." It was only a consequence of introducing legal market mechanisms. To believe that Gorbachev was a genuine reformer, one also had to believe two other things. First, that he did not understand the dynamics of Hungary in 1956 and Czechoslovakia in 1968—namely, that reform, as his predecessor Leonid Brezhnev had concluded, was tantamount to self-annihilation. And second, that Gorbachev was as good a tactician as he seemed—that he could outmaneuver the establishment opposition and pre-empt the kinds of crackdowns that had ended Communist reforms in Eastern Europe and had been Soviet leader Nikita Khrushchev's downfall.

In other words, to grasp in real time the immense impact of what Gorbachev was doing, one had to understand that the underlying threat to reform derived not from conservative opposition but from the system's unreformability, and one had to surmise that Gorbachev held the opposite (erroneous) view that successful reform was possible, but conservative opposition would try to snuff it out.

If Rouhani launches a program of far-reaching economic and political reforms—a big if—the vast majority of analysts will be dismissive. His program could well resemble window-dressing:

"streamlining" or "enhancing" clerical rule, "promoting" true Islamic values, strengthening Iran's security against the machinations of the Zionist entity, and so on. But watch for two signs. The first is rising anger and organized sabotage on the part of the conservative establishment, which would signal Rouhani's continued attempts to have his own way. The second, and more important, is socioeconomic or political developments that go beyond the reform agenda's putative intentions, which would signal that Rouhani had unleashed a process that he could no longer control.🌐

Getting to Yes With Iran

The Challenges of Coercive Diplomacy

Robert Jervis

I t might be wise for the United States to resign itself to Iran's development of nuclear weapons and to focus on deterring the Islamic Republic from ever using them. But U.S. leaders have explicitly rejected that course of action. "Make no mistake: a nuclear-armed Iran is not a challenge that can be contained," U.S. President Barack Obama told the UN General Assembly last September. "And that's why the United States will do what we must to prevent Iran from obtaining a nuclear weapon." U.S. officials have also made it clear that they consider direct military action to prevent Iran from acquiring a nuclear weapon an extremely unattractive option, one to be implemented only as a regrettable last resort.

In practice, then, that leaves only two tools for dealing with Iran's advancing nuclear program: threats and promises, the melding of which the political scientist Alexander George labeled "coercive diplomacy." To succeed in halting Iran's progress toward a bomb, the United States will have to combine the two, not simply alternate between them. It must make credible promises and credible threats simultaneously—an exceedingly difficult trick to pull

ROBERT JERVIS is Adlai E. Stevenson Professor of International Politics at Columbia University and a member of the Saltzman Institute of War and Peace Studies.

off. And in this particular case, the difficulty is compounded by a number of other factors: the long history of intense mutual mistrust between the two countries; the U.S. alliance with Iran's archenemy, Israel; and the opacity of Iranian decision-making.

The odds of overcoming all these obstacles are long. If Washington truly wants to avoid both deterrence and military action, therefore, it will need to up its game and take an unusually smart and bold approach to negotiations.

WHY COERCIVE DIPLOMACY IS HARD

The United States' recent record of coercive diplomacy is not encouraging. A combination of sanctions, inspections, and threats led Iraqi President Saddam Hussein to freeze his weapons of mass destruction program after the Gulf War, but it did not coerce him into accepting a long-term agreement. The reasons, as researchers have learned since Saddam's ouster, had to do with his motives and perceptions. The Iraqi leader not only sought regional dominance and the destruction of Israel but also worried about appearing weak to Iran, saw his survival in the wake of the Gulf War as a victory, and was so suspicious of the United States that a real rapprochement was never within reach. All this rendered ineffective the threats issued by the George W. Bush administration during the run-up to the 2003 U.S. invasion of Iraq and would likely have made promises of a reasonable settlement ineffective as well.

The Iraq case, moreover, is less an exception than the norm. Coercive diplomacy has worked on a few occasions, such as in 2003, when the Libyan leader Muammar al-Qaddafi chose to stop developing weapons of mass destruction partly as a result of pressure and reassurances from the United States. More often than not, however, in recent decades the United States has failed at coercive diplomacy even though it has had overwhelming power and has made it clear that it will use force if necessary. A succession of relatively weak adversaries, including Panama (1989), Iraq (1990 and 2003), Serbia (1998), and Taliban-ruled Afghanistan (2001), did not respond to American attempts at pressure, leading Washington to fall back repeatedly on direct military action. Coercive diplomacy did convince the military junta that ruled Haiti to step down in 1994, but only once it was clear that U.S. warplanes were already in the air. And today, Iran is hardly alone in its defiance: despite issuing many threats and promises, the United States has been unable to persuade North Korea to relinquish its nuclear arsenal or even refrain from sharing its nuclear expertise with other countries (as it apparently did with Syria).

The threats and promises the United States has used with Iran are not inherently incompatible: Washington has said it will punish Tehran for proceeding with its nuclear program but is willing to cut a deal with it should the program be halted. Logically, these components could reinforce each other, as the former pushes and the latter pulls Iran toward an agreement. But the dreary history of coercive diplomacy shows that all too often, threats and promises undercut, rather than complement, each other.

Threats can prove particularly troublesome, since if they fail, they can drive the threatening party onto a path it may not actually want to follow. U.S. President John F. Kennedy learned this lesson during the 1962 Cuban missile crisis. Kennedy was mostly, but not completely, joking when he said, on learning that the Soviet Union had stationed warheads in Cuba, "Last month I said we weren't going to [allow it]. Last month I should have said we don't care." More important, ramping up threats can undermine the chances that promises will be taken seriously. Inflicting increasing pain and making explicit threats to continue to do so can also raise questions about whether the party inflicting the pain really wants a deal and raise the domestic costs to the suffering government of making concessions.

When the United States suggests that it is willing to bomb Iran if it does not negotiate away its weapons program, it implies that the Americans believe that the costs of military action are tolerable. Although this increases the credibility of the threat, it could also lead Iran to conclude that the United States sees the costs of bombing as low enough to make military action more attractive than any outcome short of a complete Iranian surrender. Moreover, because Iran's nuclear program is at least in part driven by the Islamic Republic's desire to be able to protect itself against attack, this U.S. threat is likely to heighten the perceived danger and so increase Iran's determination not to be swayed from its current course.

This does not mean that pressure is always counterproductive. According to U.S. intelligence agencies, the Iranians halted their development of nuclear weapons in 2003, presumably in response to the menace created by the U.S. invasion of Iraq. It appears that what a U.S. diplomat once said of North Korea also applies to Iran today: "The North Koreans do not respond to pressure. But without pressure they do not respond."

WHY THIS CASE IS EVEN HARDER

Even if pressure can work, and despite the fact that threats do not need to be completely credible in order to be effective, Washington faces daunting obstacles in trying to establish the credibility of its threat to strike Iran. What is most obvious, bombing would be very costly for the Americans (which is one of the reasons why it has not yet been done). As Tehran surely understands, Washington knows that the likely results include at least a small war in the region, deepening hostility to the United States around the world, increased domestic support for the Iranian regime, legitimation of the Iranian nuclear weapons program, and the need to strike again if Iran reconstitutes it. Given such high costs, Tehran might conclude that Washington's threat to bomb is just a bluff, and one it is willing to call.

Ironically, the success of economic sanctions could further diminish the credibility of the U.S. threat of a military strike. Iranian leaders might judge that their U.S. counterparts will continue to stick with sanctions in the hopes that the pain will ultimately yield a change in Iranian policy, or they might think that U.S. officials will hold off on the unpopular and unilateral military option to avoid disrupting the relatively popular and multilateral sanctions regime.

The credibility of Washington's threat to bomb is also affected by the perceptions and intentions of Iran's rulers. Iranian leaders might fall into the trap of basing their predictions about U.S. policy on their own expectations, which might differ from the Americans'. Those Iranians with relatively benign intentions toward the United States might expect that it would be fairly easy for the Americans to live with a nuclear-armed Iran, assume their U.S. counterparts will think similarly, and thus think a preventive U.S. military strike is unlikely. More aggressive Iranian leaders, on the other hand, might take the U.S. threat to bomb more seriously, since they themselves see Iran's acquisition of a bomb to be significant and assume their American counterparts will, too. These Iranian hawks might thus see U.S. preventive military action as plausible and expect it, moreover, to be aimed at broader goals, such as regime change, rather than simply setting back the Iranian nuclear program.

The history of U.S. policy toward Iran over the past decade will also complicate the credibility of American threats. On the one hand, the United States has imposed unilateral sanctions and skillfully mustered support from the Europeans for severe international sanctions. Many Western observers were surprised by this, and the Iranian leadership probably was, too. On the other hand, the United States has not bombed Iran despite continuing Iranian defiance of UN resolutions and U.S. policies. Iran also cannot have failed to notice that the United States did not attack North Korea as it developed its nuclear weapons, even after having repeatedly issued strong threats that it would do so. Moreover, Washington has been trying to coerce Iran into giving up its nuclear program for ages now, to little avail, making it hard to instill a sense of urgency in its current efforts.

Of course, threatening to bomb Iran's nuclear facilities is not the only form of pressure the United States can exert. Washington can maintain the current punishing sanctions regime indefinitely or even strengthen it. It could conduct additional covert actions, especially cyberattacks, to slow down the Iranian nuclear program.

Because these actions are less costly to pursue than a military strike, threatening them might be more credible. But it can be more difficult to make such threats effective. The Iranians understand that they will pay a price for moving forward on the nuclear front. To change their minds, therefore, outsiders will have to threaten or inflict even greater pain than the Iranians are expecting.

HOW TO MAKE CREDIBLE THREATS

There are various ways the United States can make its threats more credible. The first is to voice them publicly and unambiguously. Obama has already gone quite far in his public statements, so the low-hanging fruit in this area has been picked. If the confrontation continues, however, a concerted campaign to inform the American public about the impending risk of war would resonate strongly, especially if capped by a congressional resolution authorizing the possible use of force against Iran. If those steps failed to sway the Iranians, the United States could issue an ultimatum, sending a clear signal to all parties that time was running out for a peaceful solution to the crisis, although doing so would be highly controversial at home and abroad and would mean giving up the military advantages of surprise.

U.S. policymakers could also stop publicly expressing their reluctance to use force and instead emphasize that they think an attack on Iran would benefit the United States. They could claim to expect that a U.S. strike would deal a dramatic blow to Iran's nuclear effort, serve as a powerful warning to other potential proliferators, strengthen the United States' global reputation for resolve, and possibly even trigger an Iranian revolution.

Private threats at this point would probably add little, but threats delivered confidentially by third parties close to Tehran, such as China and Russia, might have more credibility, and these states might carry the message if they were convinced that the only alternative was U.S. military action. Conversely, Israeli statements expressing skepticism that the United States will ever bomb Iran have undercut Washington's position. If Israeli leaders were to stop such talk and start claiming that they are now confident that the United States is willing to strike if necessary (albeit not on the timetable that Israel would prefer), such a shift would be duly noted in Tehran.

The United States could also increase the credibility of its threats by specifying the Iranian actions that would trigger an attack. The fact that Obama has resisted calls to announce such "redlines" does not mean that he does not have them. It seems likely that the decision for a strike would be made if Iran got close enough to producing a nuclear weapon that it could do so quickly and stealthily, or began producing highly enriched uranium, or expelled the International Atomic Energy Agency's inspectors. Still, even if announcing specific redlines such as these would enhance U.S. credibility, it would have downsides as well. Specifying what would be prohibited would mark out what would be permitted, and Iran could take that as an invitation to move right up to the redlines.

Washington could lend its threats credibility through actions even more than through words. It could bolster its military capabilities in a way that demonstrated its seriousness, including making expensive preparations to deal with retaliation by Iran after an American attack. It could even begin military maneuvers that have some risk of provoking Iran and leading to escalation, thus showing that Washington is not frightened by the prospect of a fight developing accidentally.

U.S. threats could also be made more credible if Washington developed plans for a strike against Iranian nuclear facilities and then deliberately allowed Iranian intelligence services to learn the details. In this scenario, the Iranians would have to believe they discovered something the Americans had sought to hide from them, lest they conclude it was simply a ruse designed to impress them. This kind of maneuver is tricky: although sound in principle, in practice it has generally proved too clever by half. During the 1961 Berlin crisis, for example, the Kennedy administration provided West Germany with its plans for a military response to the standoff, knowing the West German government had been penetrated by

Soviet intelligence. And in 1969, the Nixon administration staged an ostensibly secret nuclear-alert exercise designed to convey the strength of the U.S. commitment to South Vietnam. In both cases, however, the Soviets hardly noticed.

One might assume that the United States could increase the credibility of its threats in Iranian eyes by building up its defenses, seemingly in preparation for a possible conflict. But bulking up U.S. capabilities against Iranian missiles in the eastern Mediterranean and the Persian Gulf might also send the opposite signal—that the United States is preparing not to attack but rather to live with (and deter) a nuclear-armed Iran. Canceling the deployment of systems designed to defend against Iranian missiles, in fact, would be a strong and dramatic signal that the United States has no intention of allowing a nuclear Iran and is willing to strike preventively to head off such a prospect.

WHY IT'S HARD TO MAKE CREDIBLE PROMISES

In general, making promises credible is even harder than making threats credible, and that is especially true in this case because of the history of mutual mistrust and the conflicting historical narratives that each side tells itself. U.S. promises to Iran are complicated by other factors as well. There are multiple audiences listening in on anything Washington says to Tehran: domestic constituencies, Arab states, North Korea, other states that might seek nuclear weapons, and, of course, Israel. The fear of an Israeli attack may provide a useful source of extra pressure, but Iranian perceptions of U.S.-Israeli collusion can make U.S. signaling to Iran more difficult. American promises must be seen to cover Israeli actions as well, and some promises designed to reassure Israel of U.S. protection might conflict with conciliatory messages Washington wishes to send to Tehran.

U.S. policymakers also have limited knowledge of Iranian perceptions and domestic politics. It is generally agreed that Iran's nuclear policy rests in the hands of the country's supreme leader, Ayatollah Ali Khamenei. But it is hard to know just what his goals are, how he perceives U.S. messages, and even which messages are accurately conveyed to him. If history is any lesson, the likelihood is that he interprets much American behavior, including promises, in ways that Americans would find utterly bizarre.

Just what various Iranian actors would perceive as a reward, moreover, might be hard to determine. Some figures in or close to the regime, for example, have built fortunes and political power bases around adapting to sanctions, so removing or loosening sanctions might actually harm rather than help them. Even the most valuable prize the West could offer—the normalization of relations and the integration of the Islamic Republic into the world community— could conflict with the worldview of dominant actors in Iran, undercut their power, and be seen by them, quite possibly accurately, as a step toward eventual regime change.

All these gaps in knowledge and trust stand in the way of the United States' ability to make credible promises of any kind to Iran, whether minor assurances intended to serve as confidence-building measures or the more substantial promises that could lead to a durable diplomatic settlement. In the most likely deal, Iran would agree to stop designing warheads and to refrain from enriching uranium above the 20 percent level. It would retain only limited stockpiles of uranium enriched to 5–20 percent, accept limits on the capacities of its enrichment facilities, allow robust inspections of its nuclear facilities, and agree to refrain from building facilities that the United States could not destroy. (Such a deal would permit the heavily fortified underground Fordow enrichment plant to remain open, since it is vulnerable to a U.S. strike— something that would displease the Israelis, whose own capabilities are insufficient to overcome Fordow's defenses.)

In return, the United States would accept a limited Iranian enrichment program, promise not to try to overthrow the regime (and maybe not to undermine it), and suspend sanctions that were imposed specifically in response to the nuclear program. The United States might also restore normal diplomatic relations with Iran—although taking that step, along with lifting other sanctions, might require a larger grand bargain involving Iran's ending its support for Hamas and Hezbollah.

To convince Iran that such a deal is possible, the United States would have to surmount four barriers. It would need to gain some measure of Israeli acquiescence, both to satisfy influential pro-Israel constituencies in the United States and to convince Iran that the deal would not be undercut by Israeli sabotage, assassinations, or attacks. Accepting a civilian nuclear program in Iran would necessitate repealing or carving out some sort of exception to various UN Security Council resolutions, because the original sanctions were applied in response to the establishment of the nuclear program itself, not to the subsequent progress Iran has apparently made.

Washington would need to convince Tehran that negotiations were not designed to weaken it and that a settlement would end American efforts at regime change. Security assurances would have to be part of any deal, and they would be hard to craft. The fact that the United States helped overthrow Qaddafi in 2011 despite his earlier agreement to abandon his weapons of mass destruction program would surely be on Iranian minds.

Finally, the United States would have to find some way of offering Iran intangible goods it truly craves: respect and treatment as an equal. Not only can the process of hard bargaining get in the way of respectful treatment, but so can even the imagery used to think about such bargaining—such as talk of "carrots and sticks," which implies that Iran is an animal that the West is trying to manipulate. On the other hand, showing respect to Iran would not cost the United States a great deal.

GETTING TO THE TABLE

Although the United States and its European allies are talking with Iran now, these conversations seem to involve little more than recitations of unyielding opening positions. Distrust is often highest at the beginning of a negotiation process, since both sides fear that any preliminary concessions will not only be pocketed but also be taken as a sign of weakness that will embolden the other side to hold out for more.

There are standard, if imperfect, ways to deal with this problem, such as by using disavowable third parties who can float enticing ideas without exposing actual negotiating positions. Ambiguous "feelers" are also useful, since they require the other side to respond to a message before its true meaning is revealed and so limit the first state's exposure. But the distrust between the United States and Iran runs so deep that the normal playbook is unlikely to work here. Getting through to the supreme leader and convincing him that serious negotiations are in his interest will be difficult. Appealing to him personally and directly, in both public and private, might be effective, as might sending a high-level emissary (although such steps should be reserved until close to the last possible minute, to avoid undue humiliation should they fail).

A dramatic (if unlikely) approach would be for the United States to unilaterally suspend some of its sanctions against Iran, halt all its military preparations related to Iran, or declare that the option of using force is no longer on the table. A more plausible scenario would be for U.S. leaders to try to communicate that they are ready for an agreement by letting the Iranian regime know that they are studying how to suspend sanctions in stages and developing various forms of security guarantees.

The normal negotiating procedure would be to start with small confidence-building measures and put off dealing with the central and most difficult issues for while, until some progress and mutual trust have been achieved. It is probably too late for that, however, especially since many of the standard smaller steps have been removed from consideration by the recent application of even tougher international sanctions on Iran. Until recently, for example, a freeze-for-freeze approach to confidence building might have been possible: a U.S. offer to take no further aggressive steps in exchange for a comparable Iranian move. But at this point, given the pain the sanctions are currently inflicting, modifying them or suspending them would probably be required, which would be a much bigger concession on the part of the United States and Europe.

It will probably be necessary for Washington to sketch the broad contours of a possible final agreement before talks begin. Entering serious negotiations would carry high political costs for the White House and spark a major political struggle in Tehran—risks the leaders on each side would take only if there seemed to be good prospects of an acceptable solution. And any agreement, of course, would have to be carried out incrementally in order for each side to guard against the other's reneging.

Still, the United States may need to put more of its cards on the table at the start. It will have to convince Khamenei that successful negotiations would greatly reduce the threat to his country posed by the United States and that Washington would be willing to accept an appropriately safeguarded Iranian civilian nuclear program. There will be a strong temptation in Washington to reserve such inducements for the final stage of hard bargaining, but holding them back is likely to greatly decrease the chance that the negotiations will reach that stage at all.

The obstacles to successful negotiations may be so great that the best the United States can achieve is a form of containment that would maintain something like the status quo, with Iran remaining at some distance from a weapon. Such a situation might not be stable, however, and what Soviet Premier Nikita Khrushchev told Kennedy at the height of the Cuban missile crisis could also prove relevant to the U.S.-Iranian confrontation: "Mr. President, we and you ought not now to pull on the end of the rope in which you have tied the knot of war, because the more the two of us pull, the tighter the knot will be tied. And a moment may come when that knot will be tied so tight that even he who tied it will not have the strength to untie it. And then it will be necessary to cut that knot."

Looking carefully at the challenges of coercive diplomacy in this case is sobering. Using threats and promises to successfully manage the problems posed by Iran's nuclear program will be difficult at best, requiring extraordinary levels of calmness, boldness, creativity, and forbearance. But if Washington is determined to avoid both military action and deterrence, those are the qualities it will need to summon. 🌐

On the Road to Yes With Iran

How to Read the Nuclear Deal

Robert Jervis

There is nothing surprising about the interim deal with Iran except that it was signed. It is true that one side or the other might have gained a little more had it held out a bit longer, but the benefits would have been slight. For the West, the advantages of the arrangement are obvious: Iran will be a bit further away from gaining the capability to produce a bomb, it will find it harder to cheat in the face of increased inspections, and it will gain some limited and temporary sanctions relief. In addition, each side will have more reason to trust the other.

The objections of Israeli Prime Minister Benjamin Netanyahu and others are really less to the interim agreement than to the ultimate deal that is most likely to result. In terms of the nuclear program, any long-term agreement will look quite a bit like the current one. Although the West will not formally recognize Iran's "right to enrich," it will acknowledge its enrichment program, albeit with a number of restrictions. The details have yet to be negotiated, but limits would likely be placed on the number and type of centrifuges Iran could deploy, the level to which it could enrich uranium (to five if not 3.5 percent), and the size of the stockpile it could retain (probably about the same as now). Controls would be placed

ROBERT JERVIS is Adlai E. Stevenson Professor of International Politics at Columbia University and a member of the Saltzman Institute of War and Peace Studies.

on Iran's Arak reactor, perhaps even changing it from a heavy-water unit to a more proliferation-resistant light-water one. Inspections would be ramped up in order to give the world confidence that Iran is not enriching uranium at secret sites, and there would have to be interviews with members of the Iranian unit working on warhead design, including Mohsen Fakhrizadeh.

To be sure, success is not guaranteed, especially because of domestic politics in both the United States and Iran. Even under the best circumstances, there will be hard bargaining, especially over what sanctions should be lifted and when. Each side will seek arrangements that are relatively easy for it to reverse but lock the other side in as much as possible. If these negotiations cannot reach fruition, the interim arrangements might be extended, although they would probably have to be accompanied by some new sanctions relief, since the funds the West are now releasing will be used up in the next six months.

Whether a long-term agreement is reached or something less is patched together, the point would not be to prevent a nuclear breakout, which is impossible, but to ensure that the West would detect it in a timely manner and could disrupt it (and that Iran would understood that to be the case). This is the crucial point. The West—the world, really—needs to be confident that there would be a gap of at least two or three months between prohibited activities being detected and nuclear weapons actually appearing. Critics see this timeline as being much too short, arguing that Iranian cleverness and western fecklessness could combine to reduce it to zero, and that two or three months is not enough time to react.

The first point has more merit than the second but is less sensitive to the timeline. The response that Iran would have to fear would not be the re-imposition of sanctions, which take time to put in place and to have significant effect, but bombing. The United States could easily keep plans for such an attack at the ready. Its decision to use them, although perhaps difficult, would not have to take long. Indeed, it is not clear that bombing would be more likely if the world had plenty of advance notice. It would frighten U.S.

leaders more if Iran were months rather than years away from a nuclear bomb. Still, it is not clear whether the difference really matters. How the United States, Israel, and others would respond would be largely determined by their calculations of the gains and losses from alternative courses of action and their willpower. Additional time is not likely to produce a different response.

For those who argue that any agreement must require Iran to give up its "nuclear capacity," no window of time before Iran gets the bomb is enough. But even if the Natanz enrichment facility and others like it were destroyed, short of killing the scientists and technicians involved (and seeing that no new ones are trained), this could not be done. The program could always be re-started. The slogan that Iran should give up the bomb really just means that there should be even more time between the (re)start of the program and when bombs could be produced.

The added safety that would come from Iran dismantling its nuclear program would certainly be preferable, but one has to ask whether this is a realistic possibility. Critics of the interim agreement assert that it is. And this gets to the nub of the disagreement. Of course, proof is impossible, and the sanctions levied over the past two years have had more effect than many expected. It is noteworthy, however, that almost no experts expect that the West could put enough pressure on Iran to force it to disarm. For much of Iran's population—not only the hard-liners—the enrichment program is a symbol of the country's sovereignty, independence, and ability to stand up to the West. Given Iranian pride in the country's long history and the memories of Anglo-American indirect control during much of the twentieth century, to give in would be a humiliation and an acknowledgement that Iran could occupy only a subordinate place in the world.

It is true that countries sometimes do accept the unacceptable, and Ayatollah Ruhollah Khomeini did agree to forgo his commitment to overthrowing Saddam Hussein and end the Iran-Iraq war when he came to believe (incorrectly) that the United States would intervene militarily if he did not. Indeed, it could be argued that, if the proponents of the deal are correct that Iran has made major concessions in this round, then the appropriate conclusion is that sanctions are extraordinarily powerful and, if continued, could bring complete victory. But to refuse an agreement in the expectation that sanctions would lead Iran's current leaders to back down is to gamble against the odds.

Of course, fears about Iran are not limited to its nuclear program. Its support of Syrian leader Bashar al-Assad and Hezbollah threaten the interests and violate the values of the United States and its allies. The Islamic regime by its very nature also constitutes a threat to Saudi Arabia and the Sunni-dominated Gulf states. Most of the critics of the interim arrangement argue that it leads down the wrong path because they see increased sanctions not as a way to a better bargain but as a way to the collapse of the current regime. A permanent agreement, even if it kept Iran from gaining nuclear weapons, would lift enough of the sanctions that life in Iran would become much better and the regime would gain greater domestic support.

It is justifiable to be worried about the regime's resurgence. Sanctions have brought the Supreme Leader around to the position of making concessions because he fears for the future of his regime. And that, critics argue, is the real reason that the deal must be rejected. The association of regime change with the policies of President George W. Bush should not lead the United States to reject this argument out of hand. Although it is hard to find historical parallels or evidence in the current Iranian scene that would lead one to expect this policy to succeed, stranger things have happened.

It remains doubtful, however, that such a surprise would be in store here. The central point is that the debate over the merits of the interim agreement and the likely successor should turn on whether continued and enhanced sanctions could break Iran's will, if not lead to regime change. But if these possibilities seem remote, then the interim agreement and what is likely to follow will be good deals in an imperfect world, especially compared to bombing. 🌐

Talk Is Cheap

Sanctions Might Have Brought Rouhani to the Table, but They Won't Keep Him There

Patrick Clawson

In 2012, I argued that sanctions against Iran could succeed at bringing Tehran back to the negotiating table but that they were not a strategy in and of themselves. Occasional (and usually fruitless) talks, after all, would be no substitute for overall stability and political normalization. A more successful long-term U.S. policy, I wrote, should be geared toward building a more democratic Iran. That remains true today. As Iranian President Hassan Rouhani mounts his charm offensive at the UN General Assembly, it is worth remembering that sanctions alone did not bring about the new Iranian attitude. Nor will they be enough to guarantee Iran's cooperation in the future.

Over the last two years, the U.S. and EU sanctions regimes have scored impressive results, mostly thanks to broad international support for, and compliance with, them. Some countries, such as Canada, signed on to tight trade restrictions. Others, such as India, significantly curtailed their purchases of Iranian oil and restricted what Iran could do with the payments for that oil. All told, Iran's useable oil export revenue was around two-thirds less than it would otherwise have been this year. At about $30–$35 billion a year,

PATRICK CLAWSON is Director of Research at the Washington Institute for Near East Policy and the author or editor of numerous books and studies on Iran.

Iran's useable oil revenue now stands at a level last seen a decade ago. That has compelled the government to dip into reserves and scale back populist initiatives, such as the payments Iranians get each month to compensate for some phased-out subsidies for energy and other goods. That the country now appears ready to bargain reinforces the old Iranian adage that the Islamic Republic never gives into pressure—it only gives in to great pressure.

The sanctions, however, are not solely responsible for Iran's change in attitude. Just as important has been the increasing anger of the Iranian people at the deteriorating economic situation there, caused at least as much by the incoherent populist policies of the Ahmadinejad government as by the sanctions. A cleverer regime could have avoided the brunt of Iranian anger, turning it against the United States. But Tehran has not been able to convince the population that it should be enraged at anyone other than Iran's own hard-liners, with their unhelpful economic policies and nuclear stance. These days, Iranians' first priority is fixing the economy. And in that regard, Iranians have shown that they are not willing to continue paying the heavy price—the foregone oil revenue, the inflation, the unemployment—for the once vaunted nuclear program. In second place is restoring relations with the outside world, which means reversing isolationist policies such as restrictions on the Internet and satellite television. Even Supreme Leader Ali Khamenei, a longtime proponent of resistance rather than compromise, recently spoke about the need for "heroic flexibility."

Last, but an even more important cause of Iran's new approach, has been the strengthening of democracy in Iran. June's presidential election was by no means totally fair. But, unlike in 2009, the votes were actually counted. Results were announced many hours, not one hour, after polls closed. And rather than anointing a winner, as he did in 2009, Khamenei did nothing to stop fratricidal competition among the three main conservative candidates. When he appealed to even those Iranians opposed to the Islamic Republic to come out to vote (instead of his usual trumpeting of voting being a show of support for the regime), people got the message: This time, Khamenei would live with the people's choice from among his vetted candidates. A freer election allowed for more serious debate about the country's foreign and security policies, which had previously been taboo. The Iranian people got to hear for themselves how inflexible and unreasonable Iran's previous nuclear negotiator, Saeed Jalili, had been. All the other candidates roundly attacked his positions on nuclear negotiations.

The West had long wanted to see a serious debate inside Iran about the country's nuclear program. That debate finally happened. To be sure, sanctions raised discontent about the impact of the nuclear program, but that did not translate into Iranian policy reforms until the people were given a chance to voice their views. And that would not have happened if Khamenei had not decided to let this election play out as he did. The end result was that the people gave a strong endorsement to Rouhani, the most moderate voice. The lesson for the West is that the more democratic and free Iran gets, the better the prospects for resolving the nuclear impasse. In other words, supporting freedom in Iran is not only the morally correct thing to do, it is also the best way to get Iran to abandon its nuclear ambitions.

Rouhani is no reformer. He is a man of the system, which is why he was allowed to run in the first place. He surely wants a deal, but there has been no clear public indication of the terms to which Iran might agree. Presumably, though, Iran and the West already have a pretty good idea of what an agreement would entail on the Iranian side: accepting restrictions on enrichment, shipping most if not all enriched uranium out of the country, greater transparency, and responding to International Atomic Energy Agency queries about past activities.

However, that is only one half of the deal. The other half is what the West gives in return—specifically, in the form of sanctions relief. So far, the West, the United States in particular, has been less than forthcoming on that. Iranians should be wary: In general, the United States has been slow to ease sanctions. Whether in Libya, Myanmar (also called Burma), or Vietnam, the lifting of sanctions

once they were in place took many more years than those governments might have expected. It is sobering that the Jackson-Vanik
restrictions that were placed on the Soviet Union in 1974 because
of Moscow's limits on Jewish emigration were not lifted until 2012,
more than 20 years after those emigration limits—and the Soviet
government—ceased to exist.

Before ending sanctions, the United States usually wants more
than just a reassurance that a deal will be implemented. It wants
clear evidence that any deal will be sustained, and it wants progress
on other bilateral discussions, too. In Iran's case, this means that
Washington would want Tehran to end its support for terrorism
and its egregious human rights violations. All that is to say that
whatever sanctions relief the United States might offer after nuclear discussions begin will be quite limited. Nor is it clear that the
European Union will come to the rescue: its sanctions can only be
revoked by a unanimous decision of 28 governments.

The United States might get around the problem by offering
relief to the Iranian people even while maintaining tight restrictions on the Iranian government. Already, Washington has been
simultaneously tightening sanctions on government-linked institutions while easing rules on citizens, for instance, when it comes to
athletic competitions, donations for charity work in Iran, and sales
to Iranians of mobile phones and related software. Following a
deal, Washington could do even more to end the restrictions that
pinch Iranian citizens and private businesses, perhaps by easing
visa processing and permitting trade in consumer goods with genuinely private firms. The United States' best hope for better relations with Iran is better relations with the Iranian people, and the
United States should focus on what they need and want. Providing
modest sanctions relief for the people is only a small step toward
supporting democracy, but half a loaf is better than none. 🌑

Saved by the Deal

How Rouhani Won the Negotiations and Rescued His Regime

Suzanne Maloney

Although it was greeted with heated debate in the United States, the announcement of a landmark deal on Iran's nuclear program was met with wide approval in Iran. Cheering crowds decked in purple and green, the colors associated with the country's embattled movements for moderation and reform, met Iran's nuclear negotiators at the airport. Newspapers printed special editions with jubilant headlines. And even the stern Supreme Leader, Ayatollah Ali Khamenei, released an official statement with unusual dispatch to welcome the news and laud the diplomats who hammered out the deal.

One might think that the crowds and officials were rejoicing at the relatively meager sanctions relief meted out by a justifiably mistrustful West. Or perhaps that they were celebrating the fact that the deal left open the question of whether Iran has the right to enrich uranium. In fact, their concerns were far broader: thanks to the deal, regime moderates have started to rebalance a government that seemed on the verge of toppling only a few years ago. And, in so doing, they have confounded the world's expectations. Despite facing the most severe sanctions in history, increasing global isolation, and a recent history significant domestic unrest, Iran's revolutionary theocracy has once again navigated its way off of history's

SUZANNE MALONEY is Senior Fellow at the Saban Center for Middle East Policy at the Brookings Institution.

exit ramp. Where the country heads next, of course, remains as uncertain as ever.

Iranian President Hassan Rouhani delivered on his promise to end the nuclear impasse—and in record time, only 100 days into his presidency. His authority is now more secure than that of any of his predecessors. He leads a national unity government that boasts broad support among the country's perennially warring political establishment, the explicit backing of the supreme leader, and, now, the ecstatic support of the public as well.

The last 100 days have certainly been eventful. But the real story of Iran's transformation began in 2009, with the epic turmoil that followed the contested re-election of Mahmoud Ahmadinejad as president. The unrest left deep rifts among the insiders who had governed the Islamic Republic for the previous three decades. With an array of senior political figures in prison, and what was left of the legitimacy of Iran's elections in tatters, the regime's political base had become precariously narrow.

A slew of UN sanctions on Iran's nuclear program in 2010, which were followed by yet more punitive measures by Washington and its allies, didn't help matters. As the economy faltered, Ahmadinejad emerged as the regime's most suitable scapegoat. His repudiation by the supreme leader let loose the barely contained hostilities that divided the regime's remaining defenders. Ahmadinejad's final years in office were spent battling open subversion by the rest of the establishment as well as the spasmodic crises—hyperinflation, the currency crash, product shortages—sparked by the sanctions regime.

The infighting seemed to set Iran's revolutionary enterprise on a dead-end course, headed inescapably toward collapse or capitulation. But the country's theocracy has repeatedly demonstrated a capacity for reinvention, and, somewhere along the skid into oblivion, its old guard grabbed the wheel. Just as regime stalwarts had done at the end of the devastating war with Iraq in 1988, the revolutionaries sought salvation in moderation. During that period, the regime's foremost pragmatist, Ali Akbar Hashemi Rafsanjani, took the helm of the presidency and began to reconstruct Iran's economy and revive its frayed ties around the region. This time around, they looked to veteran power broker Rouhani, whom they believed could bridge the establishment's orthodox and liberal sides and who could be trusted to spearhead a slow-motion process of rehabilitating the regime.

In this sense, Rouhani owes his surprise election victory in June not only to the millions of Iranians who overcame their fears of a replay of 2009 to vote for him but also to an establishment that had carefully cleared the way for his dark-horse candidacy. The system's sentinels had permitted him to run a wildly iconoclastic campaign that galvanized young Iranians and unshackled an extraordinary debate over the once-sacrosanct nuclear program. Then, after his win, Rouhani was permitted to install the most forward-leaning, Western-oriented cabinet in post-revolutionary history. In speeches and press conferences, he openly staked his presidency on resolving the nuclear impasse, promising more active diplomacy and efforts to build trust and transparency. Although Iranian leaders have continued to laud their ability to withstand and evade sanctions, the cost of defiance had clearly become too much for the system to bear.

Everything that has happened since then—the foreign minister's Twitter diplomacy, Rouhani's unprecedented outreach to Barack Obama and senior U.S. officials, the preliminary nuclear deal inked on Sunday—has been part of a carefully orchestrated strategy by the regime, undoubtedly endorsed by Khamenei. And, for now, its planning seems to have paid off.

However, having successfully pivoted away from the brink will not necessarily ease the Islamic Republic's challenges. The Iranian public's overjoyed response to the political and diplomatic openings of the past five months worry the aging stalwarts of Iran's revolution. Having raised the expectations of a restless young nation with a popular president and nuclear bargain, Tehran must now deliver. Iranians want to see the fruits of these breakthroughs: the trade that will bring new jobs and economic opportunities; the easing of government repression and social restrictions; a leadership that is accountable to its people and respected abroad.

In other words, the nuclear deal is not a get-out-of-jail-free card for a failing regime; rather, Iran's internal reset and the diplomatic breakthroughs that have followed will only exacerbate the pressure from below. The millions of Iranians who thronged Rouhani's rowdy campaign rallies, who reveled in the streets after he was elected, and who celebrated the nuclear deal are watching and waiting. In case the regime's leadership missed the message, many of those who greeted the nuclear negotiators were chanting slogans in support of the candidates who led the post-election protests in 2009, men who have now endured 1000 days of shockingly brutal house arrest.

If Rouhani's government of "hope and prudence" is going to fulfill his people's expectations, then the Islamic Republic's current embrace of pragmatism must prevail over its well-honed authoritarian impulses and institutions. Nothing in Iran's post-revolutionary history gives reason for optimism about enduring moderation; past attempts by pragmatic presidents to moderate the regime were derailed by hard-liner opposition and intra-elite competition. Still, with Rouhani having been entrusted with the historic role of engineering the country's first opening to Washington (something neither Rafsanjani nor Khatami could claim), he may yet prove able to transform Iran's domestic climate.

Many players around the world have critiqued the deal. But the ebullient Iranian response to the bargain offers a reminder of the power of diplomacy. The fact that the bargain boosted the profile of the country's moderates—and put more pressure on them to deliver to the Iranian people—bolsters the case for diplomacy. We now know that Washington has long pursued diplomacy, even when the political conditions within Iran were at their worst—overtures that may have helped persuade the ever-suspicious Khamenei to initiate the quiet program of recalibration that culminated with Rouhani's election.

Additional sanctions will not break a regime whose survival instincts are second to none, and they will not inspire democratic activism among a population that sees moderation as the answer to its battered hopes. Whatever else the nuclear diplomacy may accomplish, it will at least intensify popular demands on the Islamic Republic at home.

Don't Get Suckered by Iran

Fix the Problems With the Interim Accord

Mitchell B. Reiss and Ray Takeyh

Passionate supporters of the interim accord recently negotiated between Iran and the P5+1 countries (the United States,
Russia, China, the United Kingdom, France, and Germany)
see the agreement as a landmark event paving the way for a full-
scale resolution of one of the world's most dangerous problems.
Harsh critics take the opposite view, seeing it as a modern-day
Munich paving the way for an eventual nuclear Iran. Both positions are overblown. On the plus side, the Joint Plan of Action does
place some temporary constraints on Iran's nuclear activities. But
these short-term palliative measures are embedded in a framework
of principles that may define the final agreement to Iran's definite
advantage. As negotiations proceed over what should follow the current accord, Washington should try to revisit some of interim agreement's provisions and broaden the scope of negotiations to include
Iran's sponsorship of terrorism and its systemic violation of human
rights. It would be a grave error to allow the Islamic Republic to emerge
from the negotiations with its nuclear ambitions intact, its terrorist
activities undiminished, and its people denied their basic rights.

MITCHELL B. REISS is the president of Washington College in Chestertown,
Maryland. He served as director of policy planning at the State Department
from 2003 to 2005. RAY TAKEYH is a senior fellow at the Council on Foreign
Relations.

The new Iranian leadership led by President Hassan Rouhani and Foreign Minister Mohammad Javad Zarif is made up of seasoned and cagey negotiators who have handled Iran's nuclear portfolio for decades. Their strategy has always been to concede to interim demands in order to secure principles that will favorably define a final, comprehensive agreement. In the Geneva talks this fall, Iran secured a major goal—the ability to continue to enrich uranium. After decades of wrangling, the international community has finally conceded Iran's claim that its nuclear program must have an indigenous enrichment capability. The Iranians extracted another concession as well—that the final agreement will itself be an interim one. The Joint Plan of Action stipulates that the comprehensive accord will "have a specific long-term duration to be agreed upon," after which the "Iranian nuclear program will be treated in the same manner as that of any other non-nuclear weapon state party to the NPT (Nuclear Non-Proliferation Treaty)." This means that at some point in the future, Iran may be able to construct an industrial-size nuclear infrastructure that will provide it with a nuclear breakout capacity.

As the talks proceed, the international community has an opportunity to reconsider these and other concessions. The restrictions imposed on Iran's nuclear program should be permanent and foreclose the possibility that at any point Iran can produce nuclear weapons. Among the measures that should be insisted on are the shuttering of Iran's heavy-water reactor at Arak, the closing of its fortressed enrichment installation nestled in the mountains at Fordow, and the shipping out of the country of all of its enriched uranium. Any verification agreement should include the so-called additional protocol, which gives international inspectors the right to examine any facility they deem suspect, and to do so on short notice, so that proscribed activities or equipment cannot be moved or hidden.

As a further safeguard, sanctions against Iran should be suspended rather than dismantled. The UN Security Council resolutions have provided the legal foundation that made the imposition of EU sanctions possible. These resolutions, meticulously negoti-ated over the past decade by two administrations, should not be "comprehensively lifted," as the agreement suggests, but put on hold, so that they could be resurrected quickly should Iran violate its pledges. This measure would increase the Obama administra-tion's leverage and complement the current congressional legisla-tion that would impose additional sanctions on Iran should the negotiations not end in a deal.

The non-nuclear behavior of Iran's regime, moreover, should not be excluded from arms control deliberations. Even if a nuclear deal is possible, the question remains whether this agreement will signal a genuine change in Iran's behavior. Would a non-nuclear Tehran be content to participate as a responsible member of the regional order, or would it continue to work to upend it through support for terrorist groups? The Islamic Republic routinely vio-lates UN Security Council Resolution 1559, which calls for "dis-banding and disarmament of all Lebanese and non-Lebanese mili-tias." Every time Iran dispatches arms to Hezbollah, its lethal protégé, it violates this agreement. Iran's support for other terrorist groups, particularly those attacking Israel, must also be part of the ongoing nuclear talks. Iran cannot be a custodian of sensitive nu-clear technologies while remaining the world's leading sponsor of terror.

How the Iranian regime treats its own people, meanwhile, will be another important signal as to whether it wants to become a more responsible member of the international community. The Obama administration has been reluctant to discuss Iran's abuse of its citizens for fear that it might scuttle the nuclear negotiations. Its worry is misplaced. The United States has precedent and nego-tiating leverage on its side. The precedent dates from the second term of the Reagan administration, where the full-throated affir-mation of American values accompanied a robust assertion of U.S. national security interests. As secretary of state, George Shultz never hesitated to put forth issues of human rights and the plight of imprisoned dissidents, even as he discussed deep cuts with

Moscow. Further, any long-term understanding with Iran will rest not with the mullahs but with the young people and the democracy advocates who led the ill-fated Green Revolution, and who continue to look to the United States to support their aspirations. Washington must keep faith with them by continuing to speak out against the regime's violation of human rights and by raising this issue in international forums.

Finally, to succeed in nuclear negotiations with Iran, the Western powers should be mindful of some basic realities. Iran needs an agreement more than the United States does. Its battered economy and disaffected populace constitute important leverage for its negotiating partners. There is no reason for Washington to seem more eager than Tehran to reach an agreement, and it should not fear the possibility of a negotiating breakdown if its legitimate demands are not met. The only final deal worth signing is one that promises a better future for the United States, its friends and allies in the region, and the Iranian people.🌐

Confidence Enrichment

The Nuclear Deal With Iran Was About Trust, Not Verification

Kenneth Pollack

It is difficult to judge the nuclear agreement forged last weekend in Geneva as anything other than a good deal. The Iranians will be no closer to having a nuclear breakout capability when the deal concludes than they are today. The amount of money that the Iranians will get is paltry—about $7 billion total over six months—especially compared to the roughly $30 billion that Tehran will lose during that period as a result of the sanctions on oil sales and financial transactions, all of which remain firmly in place. The objections that have been raised to the deal so far are either specious or tautological, or require the kind of tenuous conspiracy thinking that we typically disparage when it comes from the Iranians.

But the deal is only a small step in the right direction. Iran will end up somewhat farther away from developing a nuclear breakout capability, but it is hard to go much beyond that. There are so many ways for Iran to acquire the fissile material for a nuclear weapon that it is impossible to assess whether it will set Iran back by a week, a month, or a year. (Any such claims tend to reflect what the claimant wants you to believe much more than objective reality.) Moreover, the interim agreement will last for only six months and

KENNETH M. POLLACK is a senior fellow at the Brookings Institution and the author, most recently, of *Unthinkable: Iran, the Bomb, and American Strategy*.

says nothing about what will happen at the end of that period. The hope is that the two sides will use the time to craft a comprehensive follow-on agreement; but the interim deal contains only the broadest signposts for such an agreement. Three years from now, if there is no comprehensive agreement, this interim deal is going to look irrelevant—not bad, just immaterial.

In that sense, the interim deal is only important to the extent it helps to produce that ultimate, comprehensive agreement. Fortunately, the deal has real value as a confidence-building measure.

Simply put, the United States and Iran don't trust each other. That is understandable given how they have both behaved in the 34 years since the Islamic Revolution. Mistrust is so deeply rooted on both sides that it has often threatened to make any serious negotiations impossible.

What is most significant about the current deal is its potential to overcome that mutual mistrust. Both sides demonstrated a willingness to make concessions on the issues that the other side needed them to—and that is ultimately what will be necessary if there is going to be a successful final agreement. The United States needed to see the Iranians take meaningful steps to stop their pursuit of nuclear-weapons capability as reassurance that Iran was ready to give it up as part of a comprehensive agreement. Similarly, Iran needed some sign that the West (particularly the United States) would be ready to provide Tehran with meaningful sanctions relief in exchange for major concessions on its nuclear program.

That's exactly what this deal did. The Iranians agreed to halt their progress toward a nuclear breakout capability for six months. Moreover, by agreeing to dilute its existing stockpile of uranium enriched to 19.75 percent purity, Iran demonstrated its willingness to *scale back* its nuclear program and move farther away from a breakout capability—the most critical element of any comprehensive agreement. Similarly, the West showed Iran that it was willing to give Iran some cash and to suspend some sanctions, which are Iran's minimal requirements for a comprehensive agreement. It is true that the sanctions were suspended but not rescinded, and that they represented the least important of the sanctions on Iran. But the signal mattered more than the substance.

Now both sides can tell their domestic audiences that the other side demonstrated a willingness to make the kind of painful concessions that will be required for a final deal. And that should give everyone some confidence that it is possible to get a more comprehensive agreement, one that would finally end the threat posed by Iran's existing nuclear program. The interim agreement marks a very important, albeit mostly symbolic, step toward the type of deal that, not so long ago, seemed entirely unimaginable.

Caution is still in order. There are huge hurdles to be overcome. In particular, the U.S. Congress will have to allow meaningful sanctions relief to Iran, just as Iran's hard-liners are going to have to be convinced not to stand on principle when it comes to their "right" to enrich and their demand to have all sanctions lifted. The U.S. Congress is going to have to agree to allow Iran's economy to revive and Tehran's hard-liners are going to have to be satisfied with the revival of their economy and some very limited enrichment activity.

This interim accord makes it possible to imagine such a deal, but it doesn't make it a sure thing. It brings to mind the Chinese proverb that a journey of a thousand miles begins with a single step. We have finally taken that single step, and we should not ignore its importance after so many false starts. But we still have many miles to go. 🌏

Still Time to Attack Iran

The Illusion of a Comprehensive Nuclear Deal

Matthew Kroenig

Much has changed in the two years since I wrote "Time to Attack Iran," but one basic fact hasn't: diplomacy remains unlikely to neutralize the threat from Iran's nuclear program. A truly comprehensive diplomatic settlement between Iran and the West is still the best possible outcome, but there is little reason to believe that one can be achieved. And that means the United States may still have to choose between bombing Iran and allowing it to acquire a nuclear bomb. That would be an awful dilemma. But a limited bombing campaign on Iran's nuclear facilities would certainly be preferable to any attempt to contain a nuclear-armed Iran.

The successful negotiation of an interim deal between Iran and the United States and its negotiating partners has not substantially improved the chances that this problem will be resolved diplomatically. On the most important issue, the two sides are as far apart as ever, at least judging from the way that the Iranian government

MATTHEW KROENIG is an associate professor and International Relations Field Chair in the department of government at Georgetown University, a senior fellow at the Brent Scowcroft Center on International Security at the Atlantic Council, and the author of the forthcoming book *A Time to Attack: The Looming Iranian Nuclear Threat*.

still makes claims of a "right to enrich" uranium, despite the multiple U.N. Security Council Resolutions that have demanded the suspension of Iran's uranium enrichment program. Any deal that permits Iran to continue enriching uranium cannot be considered comprehensive in any sense. At present, it is estimated that Iran could dash to a nuclear weapons capability in two or three months. A deal that allows limited enrichment would push that timeline back to about six months, at best. (Some analysts, including Joseph Cirincione and Colin Kahl, have misleadingly claimed that the world still has years to solve the problem because it would take Iran a long time to develop an arsenal of deliverable warheads. But that is beside the point: Whenever the Iranian government develops bomb-grade fissile material, it can then move that material to an undisclosed location, thus taking the West's military option off the table.) In other words, the comprehensive deal under discussion would put the two sides back where they were in January 2012, when "Time to Attack Iran" was first published.

It is tempting to believe that the new atmosphere of détente between the Iranian and U.S. governments makes launching a military operation against Iran politically infeasible. In fact, a number of scenarios could trigger an attack. First, the diplomatic track might break down altogether. Congress might pass sanctions that scuttle the deal; Iranian hard-liners might do their part to undermine it; Iran's supreme leader, Ayatollah Ali Khamenei, might be unwilling to make necessary concessions; or the diplomats might simply fail to come to mutually acceptable terms. If any of these things happen and Iran resumes its nuclear activities, Washington would then have months to either use force or prepare for a nuclear-armed Iran.

Second, diplomats might fail to produce a comprehensive deal and instead settle for making the interim deal permanent. The text of the interim deal states that it is "renewable by mutual consent," but renewing the current deal would leave Iran's program perpetually two or three months away from a breakout capability—a very thin margin of error for U.S. policymakers. Any suggestion that

Iran was violating the terms of the deal would have to lead to immediate consideration of a military option.

Third, if Tehran does agree to a deal that permits enrichment, it might violate the deal's terms by quietly continuing to pursue a nuclear weapons breakout capability. Iran's leaders would like to have sanctions relief and nuclear weapons too. At present, the U.S. government and the international community are laser-focused on Iran, but once the United States formally declares an end to the Iranian nuclear crisis, its gaze will wander. Relations will be normalized, trade will resume, and global leaders will forget about Iran and start worrying about other issues. Iran may calculate that it would be difficult for the United States to rally support for new international sanctions if Iran cheats on its agreements. In the absence of renewed international pressure, the United States would be forced to consider a military option to stop Iran from building the bomb.

Fourth, even if Iran fully abides by the terms of a deal, it would only be for a limited time. The text of the interim agreement promises that the comprehensive agreement would hold for a "specified long-term duration." Early reports suggest that Iranian officials envision a three-to-five-year timeframe for a comprehensive accord, whereas the P5 plus 1 will press for 10 to 20 years. At the end of that specified time period, however long that might be, all bets would be off and Iran could resume its march to a nuclear weapons capability without violating the agreement.

Any discussion of a U.S. attack on Iran is sure to elicit opposition in the United States. But the White House would be wrong to heed the arguments of those who would voice moral objections to such an attack. If the rules that govern the international system, including the nuclear nonproliferation regime, are to have any meaning, they must be enforced. Some people are comfortable with military intervention for humanitarian reasons but place nuclear proliferation in a different category. Yet the spread of nuclear weapons poses a grave threat to international peace and security. If the United States believes that it is imperative to prevent nuclear war and stop additional countries from acquiring the world's deadliest weapons, then it must be willing, in principle, to use force to achieve that objective.

When it comes to using force to prevent nuclear proliferation, the questions are practical ones: Does the use of force have a reasonable chance of success, and is it superior to available alternatives? In some instances, such as North Korea's nuclear program today, those questions must be answered in the negative. But Iran is different. A U.S. strike, provided it is launched in time, could destroy Iran's key nuclear facilities, set Iran's nuclear program back a number of years, at a minimum, and, by changing a number of factors, including the calculations of Iran's government, create a significant possibility that Iran never acquires nuclear weapons. To be sure, there are serious risks, but they pale in comparison to the dangers of living with a nuclear-armed Iran for decades to come, the further spread of nuclear weapons in the region and around the world, and an increased risk of nuclear war against Israel and the United States.

The United States must, of course, always update its assessments in light of new evidence, but nothing that has transpired in the past two years changes the fact that a military intervention may be necessary to solve the Iranian nuclear crisis. Iran began enrichment at Fordow, a facility buried in the side of a mountain near the holy city of Qom, but the facility is no match for the United States' new and improved bunker-busting bombs. The Arab Spring toppled other governments in the region, but the Iranian regime remains strong, passing the presidency without violence or protest to a regime insider in August of this year. Iran's new president, Hassan Rouhani, is certainly less of a firebrand than Ahmadinejad, but his election would not in any way make a nuclear-armed Iran less dangerous.

The most important change in the past two years, however, is that President Barack Obama has come out forcefully on my side of this debate and against the arguments of my critics. As he has stated many times since March 2012, a nuclear-armed Iran "not a challenge that can be contained" and the United States must be prepared to do "everything required to prevent it." Many outside the Beltway express skepticism when Obama makes such threats, but his closest advisers insist that he is fully committed to preventing a nuclear arms race in the Middle East and is prepared to use force if necessary to keep Tehran from getting the bomb. Fortunately, the situation is not yet at that point. For now, everyone should hope for a satisfactory diplomatic resolution to the crisis. But, if that effort fails, no one, especially not Iran's leaders, should delude themselves about what should come next.☯

Still Not Time to Attack Iran

Why the United States Shouldn't Play Chicken With Tehran

Colin H. Kahl

In my article "Not Time to Attack Iran" (March/April 2012), I
made the case for pursuing a diplomatic solution to the Iranian
nuclear challenge, arguing that, because of the risks and costs
associated with military action, "force is, and should remain, a last
resort, not a first choice." Key developments in 2013—namely, the
election of Hassan Rouhani, a moderate, as Iran's new president
and the signing of an interim nuclear deal by Iran and the United
States and its negotiating partners—reinforce this conclusion. Whatever hawks such as Reuel Marc Gerecht or Matthew Kroenig might
argue, it is still not time to attack Iran. Indeed, the prospects for
reaching a comprehensive agreement to resolve the nuclear impasse
peacefully, while far from guaranteed, have never been brighter.

A LIGHT AT THE END OF THE TUNNEL

After decades of isolation, the Iranian regime may finally be willing to place meaningful limits on its nuclear program in exchange
for relief from punishing economic sanctions. In Iran's June 2013
presidential election, Rouhani handily defeated a slate of conservative opponents, including the hard-line nuclear negotiator Saeed

COLIN H. KAHL is an associate professor in the Security Studies Program in
the Edmund A. Walsh School of Foreign Service at Georgetown University.

Jalili, who had campaigned on continuing Iran's strategy of "nuclear resistance." Rouhani, in contrast, pledged to reach a nuclear accommodation with the West and free Iran from the economic burden imposed by sanctions. Rouhani, also a former nuclear negotiator, believes he has the support of the Iranian people and a green light from Supreme Leader Ayatollah Ali Khamenei to reach a comprehensive nuclear accord with the United States and the other members of the P5+1 (Britain, China, France, Germany, and Russia).

The first step on the road to a comprehensive deal came in November 2013 with an interim agreement in Geneva, in which Tehran agreed to freeze and modestly roll back its nuclear program in exchange for a pause in new international sanctions and a suspension of some existing penalties. The deal represents the most meaningful move toward a denuclearized Iran in more than a decade. It neutralizes Iran's stockpile of 20 percent uranium and therefore modestly lengthens Iran's "breakout" timeline—the time required to enrich uranium to weapons grade—by one or two months. A new inspections regime also means any breakout attempt would be detected soon enough for the international community to react, and expanded International Atomic Energy Agency (IAEA) access to Iran's nuclear infrastructure will make it more difficult for Iran to divert critical technology and materials to new secret sites. The terms also preclude the new plutonium reactor at Arak from becoming operational, halting the risk that Iran could soon use plutonium to build a bomb.

For all its good points, the interim agreement does not by itself resolve the Iranian nuclear challenge. Rather, the accord is designed to create at least a six-month diplomatic window (the initial period of the agreement), or longer if the agreement is extended, to negotiate a final, comprehensive solution. At the very least, U.S. officials have suggested that the ultimate deal must permanently cap Iran's enrichment at five percent; substantially reduce Iran's low-enriched uranium stockpile; place significant limits on the number of Iranian centrifuges and enrichment facilities; dismantle Arak or convert it to a proliferation-resistant light-water reactor;

allow much more intrusive inspections of both declared and undeclared facilities; and account for the "past military dimensions" of Iran's nuclear research. In exchange, Iran would receive comprehensive relief from multilateral and national nuclear- and proliferation-related sanctions.

GOING FOR BROKE

Some analysts argue that U.S. negotiators should use the leverage created by crippling economic sanctions and Iran's apparent willingness to negotiate to insist on a total dismantling of Iran's fuel-cycle activities. The maximalist approach is reflected in Israeli Prime Minister Benjamin Netanyahu's stated requirements for a final deal: no uranium enrichment at any level, no stockpile of enriched uranium, no centrifuges or centrifuge facilities, and no Arak heavy-water reactor or plutonium reprocessing facilities.

Attempting to keep Iran as far away from nuclear weapons as possible seems prudent and reasonable. It is imperative that any final deal prohibits Iran from possessing facilities that would allow it to produce weapons-grade plutonium, for example. But in reality, the quest for an optimal deal that requires a permanent end to Iranian enrichment at any level would likely doom diplomacy, making the far worse outcomes of unconstrained nuclearization or a military showdown over Tehran's nuclear program much more probable. Regardless of pressure from the United States, its allies, and the wider international community, the Iranian regime is unlikely to agree to end all enrichment permanently.

Khamenei, the ultimate decider on the nuclear file, has invested far too much political capital and money (more than $100 billion over the years) in mastering enrichment technology and defending Iran's nuclear rights (defined as domestic enrichment). The nuclear program and "resistance to arrogant powers" are firmly imbedded in the regime's ideological raison d'être. So, even in the face of withering economic sanctions, Khamenei and hard-liners within the Revolutionary Guard are unlikely to sustain support for further negotiations—let alone acquiesce to a final nuclear deal—if the end result reflects a total surrender for the regime. As Alireza Nader, an Iran analyst at the RAND Corporation, observes, "[S]anctions are a danger to their rule, but weakness in the face of pressure might be no less a threat."

Nor are Rouhani and his negotiating team likely to agree to halt enrichment or advocate for such a policy, since doing so would be political suicide. In 2003, during Rouhani's previous role as Iran's chief nuclear negotiator, he convinced Khamenei to accept a temporary suspension of enrichment. But further talks with the international community stalled in early 2005 over a failure to agree on Iran's asserted right to enrichment, and Tehran ended its suspension shortly thereafter. Rouhani is unlikely to let that happen again.

PLAYING CHICKEN
Given the certainty that Iran will reject maximalist demands from the United States, the United States should only make such demands if it is willing to go to the brink of the abyss with Iran, escalating economic and military threats to the point at which the regime's survival is acutely and imminently in danger. Yet pursuing such a high-risk strategy is unlikely to succeed, and the consequences of failure would be profound.

First, it is unclear whether any escalation of sanctions could bring the regime to its knees in time to prevent Iran from achieving a breakout capability. Iran's apparent willingness to negotiate under pressure is not, in and of itself, evidence that more pressure will produce total surrender. Iran's economy is in dire straits, but the country does not appear to be facing imminent economic collapse. Khamenei and the Revolutionary Guard also seem to believe that the Islamic Republic weathered far worse during the Iran-Iraq War, an eight-year conflict that killed hundreds of thousands of Iranians and produced over half a trillion dollars in economic losses before Iran agreed to a cease-fire. Even if Washington goes forward with additional sanctions, economic conditions are not likely to produce enough existential angst among Iranian leaders, generate mass unrest, or otherwise implode the regime before Iran achieves a nuclear breakout capability. And even if they did lead to regime change, it still might not prove sufficient to force a nuclear surrender. After all, the imprisoned leaders of the Green Movement and Iranian secularists opposed to the Islamic Republic, as well as a significant majority of the Iranian people, also support Iran's declared right to enrichment.

Second, and somewhat paradoxically, ramping up sanctions to force regime capitulation now could end up weakening international pressure on Iran. For better or worse, Rouhani has already succeeded in shifting international perceptions of Iran. If the United States, rather than Iran, comes across as intransigent, it will become much more difficult to maintain the international coalition currently isolating Tehran, particularly on the parts of China, Russia, and numerous other European and Asian nations. Some fence sitters in Europe and Asia will start to flirt with Iran again, leaving the United States in the untenable position of choosing between imposing extraterritorial sanctions on banks and companies in China, India, Japan, South Korea, Turkey, and elsewhere, or acquiescing to the erosion of the international sanctions architecture.

Third, issuing more explicit military threats (through public warning by U.S. President Barack Obama or congressional passage of a resolution authorizing the use of military force, for example) is also unlikely to achieve a maximalist diplomatic outcome. There is little doubt that maintaining a credible military option affects the Iranian regime's calculations, raising the potential costs associated with nuclearization. And if diplomacy fails, the United States should reserve the option of using force as a last resort. But threats to strike Iranian nuclear sites surgically, no matter how credible, would not create a sufficient threat to the survival of the regime to compel it to dismantle its nuclear program completely.

Finally, attempting to generate an existential crisis for the Islamic Republic could backfire by increasing the regime's incentives to acquire nuclear weapons. If the United States escalates economic or military pressure at the very moment when Iran has finally begun to negotiate in earnest, Khamenei will likely conclude that the real and irrevocable goal of U.S. policy is regime change. Solidifying this perception would enhance, rather than lessen, Tehran's motivation to develop a nuclear deterrent. In short, playing chicken with Iran will not work and is likely to result in a dangerous crash. Gambling everything by insisting on an optimal deal could result in no deal at all, leaving Iran freer and potentially more motivated to build atomic arms and making a military confrontation more likely.

STILL TIME FOR DIPLOMACY

During a December 2013 forum hosted by the Brookings Institution, Obama said, "It is in America's national security interests . . . to prevent Iran from getting a nuclear weapon. . . . But what I've consistently said is, even as I don't take any options off the table, what we do have to test is the possibility that we can resolve this issue diplomatically." When asked by a former Israeli general in the audience what he would do if diplomacy with Iran breaks down, Obama said, "The options that I've made clear I can avail myself of, including a military option, is one that we would consider and prepare for."

Given the dangers associated with a nuclear-armed Iran, Obama is right to keep the military option alive. But he is also right to strongly prefer a diplomatic outcome. Leadership changes in Tehran and the diplomatic momentum created by the Geneva interim accord mean that there is a real chance that the Iranian nuclear crisis—a challenge that has haunted the international community for decades—could finally be resolved peacefully. No one can say for sure how high the odds of success are. But given the enormous dangers associated with both an Iranian bomb and the bombing of Iran, it is imperative to give diplomacy every chance to succeed. ❧

Befriend the Scientists

How to Bring Iran's Nuclear Program Into the Fold

Jacques E. C. Hymans

The recent international agreement on Iran's nuclear program is a welcome triumph of hope over experience. Iran's new president, Hassan Rouhani, has signaled his willingness to go further than any previous Iranian leader to satisfy the international community's concerns about his country's ultimate nuclear ends. For Rouhani and his team of political moderates, however, getting to yes with the United States and its partners is the comparatively easy part. The really tough part will be the struggle inside Iran.

The Islamic Republic's secretive nuclear program has been grinding away for nearly three decades. During this time, the country has gradually built up considerable political, technical, and organizational inertia toward the bomb. That inertia will not dissipate simply because diplomats shook hands in Geneva. What is really necessary is a profound change in the nuclear program's organizational culture—and such transformations always take time.

Given the realities of Iran's internal situation, the United States must show forbearance and reject calls to jettison the Geneva agreement at the first hint of Iranian noncompliance. Iran must be held to its promises, of course, but not in a manner that weakens

JACQUES E. C. HYMANS is Associate Professor of International Relations at the University of Southern California. He is the author, most recently, of *Achieving Nuclear Ambitions: Scientists, Politicians, and Proliferation.*

the power or resolve of the very people who have the strongest interest in keeping those promises.

Patience is merited in this case because the potential benefits far outweigh the potential costs. Even if Rouhani—contrary to all indications—really is the "wolf in sheep's clothing" that Israeli Prime Minister Benjamin Netanyahu has alleged him to be, the fact is that Israeli intelligence itself has acknowledged that Iran could not possibly have its first bomb before 2015 or 2016. Moreover, given the pathetic track record of past such estimates, in the real world an Iranian drive toward the bomb would probably need much more time than that. At this point, therefore, the United States and its partners can certainly afford to give Rouhani the benefit of the doubt.

THE CHALLENGE OF REFORM

Historically, some countries have been able to allay Western fears about their nuclear programs practically overnight. For instance, in 2003, Libyan leader Muammar al-Qaddafi had a change of heart and put his 30-year-old nuclear weapons project completely out of business within weeks.

But Iran is not Libya. For one thing, the Iranian president does not have Qaddafi's power. He has to push his policies through a maze of decision making bodies with overlapping jurisdictions and different political colorations, while constantly looking over his shoulder at Supreme Leader Ayatollah Ali Khamenei—who is not fully in command himself. Iran's many institutional bottlenecks will offer the nuclear program's old guard, aided and abetted by the country's powerful hard-line nationalist political factions, ample opportunities to resist any concessions made at the bargaining table in Geneva.

Rouhani's task is made even more complicated by the fact that the Iranian nuclear program is much bigger, more advanced, and more fundamental to national identity than Libya's was. The Iranian masses are proud of their nation's technical accomplishments, even if the hundred billion-dollar price tag seems a little steep.

Meanwhile, the program serves as an important source of income for thousands of people, many of them with political connections. This combination of concentrated benefits and diffuse costs has long tilted the political playing field in favor of Iran's nuclear priesthood.

Rouhani's greatest challenge, however, will be to ensure that his high-level policy changes are actually implemented on the ground. Bureaucrats the world over have a strong instinctive preference for keeping things just as they are, and there is no reason to think that those who have been running Iran's nuclear program are any different. Moreover, the Iranian nuclear program is not a single bureaucratic silo but rather a sprawling estate with many players and moving parts, and many secrets that the players want to hide—including from each other. Even assuming that Rouhani genuinely wants nuclear transparency, therefore, the international inspectors will inevitably face many frustrations over the next six months and beyond. Important documents they want to examine will go missing; key people they want to interview will clam up or fade into the woodwork; and when they do uncover new evidence of illicit behavior, program officials will attempt to whitewash it.

The historical case of Argentina shows just how hard it can be even for a country's own government to bring about profound change in a well-established nuclear program. In 1983, Raúl Alfonsín became the country's first democratically elected president after years of brutal military rule. Just before Alfonsín's inauguration, the military-protected Comisión Nacional de Energía Atómica revealed that it had successfully enriched uranium in a secret facility in the Andes. Although he put on a brave face in public, Alfonsín was shocked by the news and strongly suspected that the facility might be part of a broader secret bomb program.

Alfonsín sent a team of experts to investigate, but they were stonewalled. They were finally able to collect the information they needed only after the president's heavy personal intervention and three months of hard digging. Perhaps the most surprising part of this story is that, although the nuclear program's bureaucrats had made every effort to protect their secrets, in fact their real self-interest lay in coming clean; the investigative commission concluded that the enrichment plant was not part of a broader drive toward a nuclear bomb, and Alfonsín ended up providing strong support for the plant's continued operation.

In the coming months, Iranian nuclear program officials will resist opening their cupboards at least as strenuously as their counterparts in Argentina once did. But, like Alfonsín, Rouhani is no pushover. Before the Geneva negotiations even started, the president was quietly arranging the chess pieces for his reform bid. His political allies are now ensconced in key positions at the top of the nuclear estate, and Iranian hard-liners have begun to complain about "widespread human-resources changes at the nuclear facilities." These are very positive signs. Even so, the domestic battle over Iran's nuclear future has only just begun.

ATOMS FOR PEACE

Beyond maintaining realistic expectations about how fast Rouhani can change Iran's nuclear behavior, the United States should also look for ways to help him do it. The promised economic sanctions relief will surely be welcome in Iran. The real key to a permanent resolution of this crisis, however, is to convince Iran's nuclear scientific and technical workers to become not just the object of reform efforts but their driver. If the nuclear program staff themselves were sold on the promise of reform, then Rouhani and his team would be able to start sailing with the wind instead of against it.

A cultural transformation inside Iran's nuclear bureaucracy is not an impossible dream. Although the inner workings of the Iranian nuclear program remain mysterious, historical experience both inside and outside the country suggests that many of the program's scientific and technical staff have been straining at the yoke of autocratic mismanagement and want to be part of the international scientific community. It is terribly demoralizing to work in an organization that privileges ideological agendas and political timetables over professional norms. The many honorable people who are currently trapped in this situation have ample motives to become front line troops in the process of cultural change.

In line with this objective, the United States should immediately start promoting the development of collaborative relationships between American and Iranian universities and research institutions, including laboratories that have links with the nuclear program. The risk to the United States that the Iranians might learn some dangerous technical secrets from such exchanges is minor in comparison with the value to the United States of demonstrating to them that there is a bright future in store for a professionalized Iranian scientific establishment that embraces international norms. The reintegration of Iranian researchers into the global scientific community would also produce the right conditions for mutual trust and the eventual disclosure of Iran's own technical secrets. For its part, Iran would undoubtedly welcome such a bridge-building initiative.

Of course, efforts to reach out to Iranian scientists and engineers will not succeed unless the United States simultaneously puts a stop to Israel's alleged assassination campaign against these people, which has probably been counterproductive in any case.

The United States should do what it can to encourage the Iranian nuclear program to open up. Yet there is still no getting around the fact that the major responsibility for achieving that end lies with the Iranian government itself. And unfortunately, Rouhani's currently enormous stock of domestic political capital will likely soon start diminishing. As it does, the nuclear old guard may come roaring back in.

The United States should carefully prepare for the possibility that Rouhani will ultimately fail. But it should not assume that failure is his destiny. Back in the 1980s, many analysts assumed that Alfonsín would be unable to reform Argentina's nuclear estate. But he proved them wrong. Argentina's nuclear program itself embraced his policy of gradual opening, and the international community kept its cool even though Buenos Aires continued to refuse to join the Nonproliferation Treaty all the way up to 1995. Today,

Argentina is a highly respected and successful exporter of nuclear research reactors, for which it can also supply the enriched uranium fuel. And nobody suspects that its enrichment work is part of a secret nuclear weapons breakout plan. If Rouhani keeps his course and the West keeps its patience, there is a good chance that Argentina's nuclear present will be Iran's nuclear future. ✪

Pushing Peace

How Israel Can Help the United States Strike a Deal With Iran— And Why It Should

Trita Parsi

The moment that Israeli Prime Minister Benjamin Netanyahu hoped he could avoid is fast approaching: high-level negotiations between the United States and Iran that could lead to a deal that ends the decade-long standoff over Tehran's nuclear program. As Obama has welcomed the new approach of Iran's new president, Hassan Rouhani, and taken concrete steps to test Tehran's sincerity, Netanyahu has been quick to dismiss Rouhani and call for more sanctions. It is increasingly clear that Netanyahu ultimately fears the success of diplomacy, not its failure. But Israel, and its national security establishment, should not see a diplomatic resolution to the Iranian nuclear standoff as a threat.

Contrary to Israel's public line, Netanyahu's worry is not that the Iranians would cheat on any agreement, or that Rouhani would prove to be a "wolf in sheep's clothing." Rather, Netanyahu and much of Israel's security establishment view the status quo—ever-increasing sanctions that cripple Iran's economy, combined with the ever-present threat of war—as preferable to any realistic diplomatic deal.

As Israelis well know, a compromise would probably allow for limited enrichment on Iranian soil under strict verification, and the

TRITA PARSI is the founder and current president of the National Iranian American Council, and author, most recently, of *Treacherous Alliance*.

lifting of nuclear-related sanctions. Although Iran would techni-
cally remain a non–nuclear weapons state, it would be considered a
virtual nuclear power. And that, Netanyahu calculates, is sufficient
to shift the balance of power in the region to Israel's detriment,
reducing the Jewish state's maneuverability and the usefulness of
its own deterrent. There is reason to believe, then, that Israel's in-
sistence on zero enrichment is aimed to ensure that no deal is
struck at all.

Israel also understands that a resolution to the nuclear standoff
would significantly reduce U.S.-Iranian tensions and open up opportunities for collaboration between the two former allies. Since
U.S.-Iranian fellow feeling will not be accompanied by a propor-
tionate reduction in Iranian-Israeli hostilities, Israel will be left in
a relatively worse position. This is what Israelis refer to as the fear
of abandonment—that, once the nuclear issue is resolved or contained, Washington will shift its focus to other matters while Israel
will be stuck in the region facing a hostile Iran, without the United
States by its side.

These fears have been the basis of Israel's uncompromising position for the past several years. But Netanyahu has been particularly inflexible, breaking even past precedents of nimbleness. Israel
generally opposes and seeks to prevent U.S.-Iranian talks whenever possible, but swiftly shifts to a neutral position once talks are
deemed unstoppable. That way, it can still influence the agenda.

For instance, in 1999, the Clinton administration was intrigued—
according to some Israelis, "infatuated"—with the election of reformist President Mohammad Khatami, who spoke of his desire to
break the "wall of mistrust" with the United States. Israeli Prime
Minister Ehud Barak wanted neither to be locked out of a potential
dialogue nor to come across as beating the war drum when the
Clinton administration seemed intent on dialogue. To signal his
government's shift, Barak altered the status of Iran from enemy to
threat, indicating, as Israeli diplomats argued, that the current Israeli position holds that Israel does not have a conflict with the
Iranian people, the state of Iran, or with Islam. Moreover, Israel

unofficially condemned a terrorist attack targeting a member of Khatami's government.

Barak enjoyed this flexibility because he had consistently rejected the idea—and continues to do so today—that Iran constitutes an existential threat to Israel. Netanyahu, on the other hand, has come to personify the argument that he made in a 2006 address to delegates at the United Jewish Communities General Assembly: "It's 1938 and Iran is Germany." Netanyahu has painted himself— and Israel—into a corner. And rather than trying to get out, he has, at every turn, doubled down on the strategy of intransigence.

Israel needs to show nimbleness now more that ever. With Egypt, Iraq, Libya, and Syria all in various states of chaos, Iran appears to be the most resolvable challenge that the United States faces in the Middle East, and Obama seems to know it. By personally taking ownership of reaching out to Iran by seeking a meeting with Rouhani and later calling him, he has demonstrated the political will to move things forward. And Rouhani seems ready to meet the challenge. By contrast, Netanyahu's knee-jerk rejection feeds the perception that Israel—not Iran—is the chief stumbling block. Ultimately, even short of a nuclear agreement, that impression can help Iran break out of its isolation and delegitimize the sanctions regime suffocating its economy.

Beyond the perception of it, Israel has much to gain from shifting its stance on negotiations. In private conversations last year after the successful round of talks in Istanbul, Israeli strategists revealed that Israel's central concern was not enrichment but, rather, that any U.S. deal with Iran entail a "sweeping attitude change" in Tehran vis-à-vis Israel. In short, Israel did not want Washington to resolve its issues with Iran unless Iran was forced to address Israel's concerns as well—first and foremost, an Iranian de facto acceptance of Israel's right to exist.

This is precisely why diplomacy serves Israel better than Netanyahu's naysaying: Iran's position on Israel is far more likely to change in the direction Israel desires if U.S.-Iranian relations improve and the first tangible steps are taken to rehabilitate Iran into the region's political and economic structures.

Since its inception, the Iranian theocracy has adopted harsh and venomous rhetoric about Israel to boost Tehran's credibility on the Arab street and to bridge the region's Arab-Persian and Sunni-Shia divide. But Tehran's ideological impulses have not always driven policy. When ideology and geostrategic goals don't match up, Iran favors the latter. During the Iraq-Iran War, Iran and Israel quietly collaborated behind the scenes for this very reason.

Over the last two decades, Tehran's ideological and strategic imperatives have been in harmony. Strategically, Iran opposes Israel's efforts to permanently isolate it. Ideologically, the anti-Israeli card has often been helpful to create common cause with the Arab masses and to help overcome Iran's own tensions with its Sunni and Arab neighbors. When sectarian strife rises in the region, so does the utility of the anti-Israeli card for Tehran.

Improved U.S.-Iranian relations, with tangible steps to end Iran's isolation on the condition that it shifts its behavior, could divorce Iran's ideological and strategic impulses. If that happens, Iran would have compelling incentives to disentangle itself from anti-Israeli hostilities.

The Rouhani government—and its team of foreign policy practitioners, including Javad Zarif, the foreign minister—have long been inclined toward negotiations. It was this same team that in 2003 prepared the so-called grand bargain proposal, which the Bush administration chose to ignore. As part of that grand bargain, Iran said that it was willing to significantly restrain Hezbollah, Hamas, and Islamic Jihad, and even sign on to the 2002 Saudi peace plan, which offered the recognition of Israel by every country in the Muslim world in return for an Israeli recognition of a Palestinian state. That would indeed have been a "sweeping attitude change" for Iran.

Similarly, Rouhani is believed to support the concept of adopting a "Malaysian profile," which gained support during the Khatami era. The idea was that Tehran would, in return for an end to

Israeli and American efforts to isolate Iran, assume a position on Israel similar to that of Malaysia: Iran would not recognize Israel but would limit its criticism of Israel to the plight of the Palestinian population, and would avoid getting itself entangled in activities against the Jewish state. The two rivals would also recognize each other's respective spheres and disengage from further hostilities. This would have an immediate impact on Israel's tensions with Hezbollah.

That plan is not perfect—nor is it Israel's ideal relationship with Iran. But neutralizing Iran's interest in fanning anti-Israeli sentiment would be no small gain and would significantly enhance Israel's security and political position. Recognizing that, Israel should moderate its rhetoric and stop encouraging Congress to undermine diplomacy through additional sanctions. By doing so, Israel can both help diplomacy and ensure that the final outcome of the talks addresses key Israeli security concerns.

Although there is no guarantee that diplomacy will succeed, all other options suffer from the same uncertainty, particularly a military option. If anything, the risks facing Israel, especially the risk of its being "abandoned" by the United States, only increase the more Netanyahu portrays himself as unappeasable.

Bibi the Bad Cop

Can Israel Prevent a Deal With Iran?

Elliott Abrams

Most of the world is applauding the thaw between the United States and Iran. Then there are the Arabs and Israelis. Their reaction is dread, and with good reason: neither trusts U.S. President Barack Obama to prevent Iran from acquiring a nuclear weapon or from at least acquiring the capability to produce one. Israel, which has a wide base of political support in the United States, will try to stymie any nuclear deal it sees as too lenient—but that won't be easy.

In his speech to the UN General Assembly on Tuesday, Israeli Prime Minister Benjamin Netanyahu delivered messages that few wanted to hear. He reminded the world that the Iranians have lied before, warned that they may well be lying still, and claimed that they have done nothing to earn credibility. He said that Iran should first be made to comply with the International Atomic Energy Agency and UN resolutions, which it has defied for decades—most notably by developing clandestine, unsafeguarded sites and by continuing the enrichment of uranium. Netanyahu is setting forth standards for a nuclear agreement that are far tougher than the Obama administration believes can be negotiated and, as a result, are not even being sought.

The hard part for Israel comes next, when the world's leaders have returned home. The recent debate over Syria—when the administration backed away from using force, Congress seemed on

ELLIOTT ABRAMS is Senior Fellow for Middle Eastern Studies at the Council on Foreign Relations and a former U.S. Deputy National Security Adviser.

the verge of voting against the use of force, and opinion polls showed the public against any military involvement—has seriously undermined the credibility of the U.S. military option. What will Israel's approach be in the coming months, when Washington's position—whatever its rhetoric—has moved from "all options are on the table" to a blind pursuit of diplomacy?

The first thing the Israelis will do is repeat, over and over again, their arguments against trusting Iranian President Hassan Rouhani. They will remind U.S. and EU officials, journalists, and anyone who will listen that he is not a reformer but a regime stalwart who, as secretary of Iran's Supreme National Security Council, had the job of buying time for the nuclear weapons program.

Second, they will make the case that any deal should have very tough standards. In this sense, Israel will be forced to be the bad cop, and to enlist other bad cops in Europe and in the U.S. Congress. If Israel had its way, Iran would have to fully account for its past (secret) work on a warhead, stop its centrifuges, stop enriching uranium and ship its existing stockpiles out of the country, prove it has no alternate route to nuclear weapons through plutonium work at the Arak facility, dismantle the underground site at Fordow, and cease the conversion of first-generation centrifuges to more efficient second-generation ones. It seems very unlikely that the United States and the other P5+1 countries will, for one thing, demand an end to all enrichment inside Iran; on all these conditions, in fact, compromise is more likely than the fulfillment of Israel's demand that all nuclear activities stop. If a full stop to the Iranian program is judged by Washington to be unattainable, Netanyahu will argue that Iran should be held to its own claim that it needs nuclear technology for nuclear power; in that case, it would need only uranium enriched to about 3.5 percent, very few centrifuges (and those in one location that is declared and inspected), and only a tiny stock of enriched uranium.

Third, Israel will ask that sanctions be strengthened, and that the Obama administration not be allowed so many waivers to permit other countries to flout the sanctions regime, until Iran actually changes its conduct—not just promises to change it. That is, sanctions should be reduced in the coming months only in exchange for Iran's exporting enriched uranium, warehousing centrifuges, and providing truthful information about the military aspects of its nuclear program.

Finally, Netanyahu will ask that the military option be strengthened, not weakened. Here, Washington's rhetoric matters, but it could do far more to bolster the now-diminished credibility of its threat to use force by carefully leaking information about U.S. military preparations or by positioning forces so that they could strike Iran should it be necessary. But the Israelis may guess that they won't get much here, so a more promising line may be to ask Washington to help them enhance their own capabilities—by providing more bunker-buster bombs and more air refueling tankers. The idea would be to demonstrate that, at least for Israel, all options are in fact on the table, and that the Americans like it that way.

The first three steps could be taken without the approval of the Obama administration—in fact, they are steps meant to limit U.S. flexibility. The fourth step would require the Obama administration's approval and action. If Israel plays its cards right, it might be able to convince Washington to help with the fourth step by promising to refrain from the first three. That is, Israel could say it can live with the possibility of Iranian cheating and moving closer to a bomb only if its own military option grows stronger.

Israel does retain one option for stymying the negotiations if they appear to be heading for what Israelis would view as a bad deal, one that would allow Iran to escape sanctions and creep closer to a bomb. That is for Israel to attack Iranian nuclear sites. Its ability to do so is already being narrowed considerably by the diplomatic thaw, because it is one thing to bomb Iran when it appears hopelessly recalcitrant and isolated and quite another to bomb it when much of the world—especially the United States—is optimistic about the prospect of talks. A window for an Israeli attack might open up if the talks bogged down and Western negotiators suggested that the Iranians were refusing to compromise, perhaps speculating that the Supreme Leader and the Revolutionary Guards did not want a deal after all. But Rouhani and his foreign minister, Mohammad Javad Zarif, are probably too smart to allow such pessimism to creep into Western ranks.

In short, the Israelis find themselves in a far worse position now than they have been for several years. There was no way for them to avoid this situation other than attacking last year; bombing Iran when Mahmoud Ahmadinejad was president would have been more defensible in the court of global public opinion. Now they must fix bleak smiles to their lips and say that they hope for the best—all the while wringing their hands about the likely terms of the deal. Given that Israel may have little ability to persuade the Western negotiators to be tough, its best path for now is to appeal to Americans, especially in Congress, to refuse to lift sanctions until Iran makes significant concessions.

Here, the Syria episode might actually help Israel, since it increased mistrust about the Obama administration's handling of foreign policy, even among Democrats. Refusing to lift sanctions and adopting tougher rhetoric toward Iran would not be partisan issues. Plenty of Democrats think that those actions are both good politics and good policy.

The Israelis have a difficult task ahead. They do not wish to play the bad cop role in an American game with Iran—and, in fact, the metaphor is misleading. In the good cop/bad cop routine, both officers are on the same team and are carefully coordinating their approaches. In this case, the Israelis fear, the bad cop wants to see the criminals jailed, and the good cop is open to a sweet plea bargain. If that's what the Iranians get, they will sit back and smile while the United States and Israel end up in a bitter argument.

Most of the world is applauding the thaw between the United States and Iran. Then there are the Arabs and Israelis. Their reaction is dread, and with good reason: neither trusts U.S. President Barack Obama to prevent Iran from acquiring a nuclear weapon or from at least acquiring the capability to produce one. Israel, which has a wide base of political support in the United States, will try to stymie any nuclear deal it sees as too lenient—but that won't be easy.

In his speech to the UN General Assembly on Tuesday, Israeli Prime Minister Benjamin Netanyahu delivered messages that few wanted to hear. He reminded the world that the Iranians have lied before, warned that they may well be lying still, and claimed that they have done nothing to earn credibility. He said that Iran should first be made to comply with the International Atomic Energy Agency and UN resolutions, which it has defied for decades—most notably by developing clandestine, unsafeguarded sites and by continuing the enrichment of uranium. Netanyahu is setting forth standards for a nuclear agreement that are far tougher than the Obama administration believes can be negotiated and, as a result, are not even being sought.

The hard part for Israel comes next, when the world's leaders have returned home. The recent debate over Syria—when the administration backed away from using force, Congress seemed on the verge of voting against the use of force, and opinion polls showed the public against any military involvement—has seriously undermined the credibility of the U.S. military option. What will Israel's approach be in the coming months, when Washington's position—whatever its rhetoric—has moved from "all options are on the table" to a blind pursuit of diplomacy?

The first thing the Israelis will do is repeat, over and over again, their arguments against trusting Iranian President Hassan Rouhani. They will remind U.S. and EU officials, journalists, and anyone who will listen that he is not a reformer but a regime stalwart who, as secretary of Iran's Supreme National Security Council, had the job of buying time for the nuclear weapons program.

Second, they will make the case that any deal should have very tough standards. In this sense, Israel will be forced to be the bad cop, and to enlist other bad cops in Europe and in the U.S. Congress. If Israel had its way, Iran would have to fully account for its past (secret) work on a warhead, stop its centrifuges, stop enriching uranium and ship its existing stockpiles out of the country, prove it has no alternate route to nuclear weapons through plutonium work at the Arak facility, dismantle the underground site at Fordow, and cease the conversion of first-generation centrifuges to more efficient second-generation ones. It seems very unlikely that the United States and the other P5+1 countries will, for one thing, demand an end to all enrichment inside Iran; on all these conditions, in fact, compromise is more likely than the fulfillment of Israel's demand that all nuclear activities stop. If a full stop to the Iranian program is judged by Washington to be unattainable, Netanyahu will argue that Iran should be held to its own claim that it needs nuclear technology for nuclear power; in that case, it would need only uranium enriched to about 3.5 percent, very few centrifuges (and those in one location that is declared and inspected), and only a tiny stock of enriched uranium.

Third, Israel will ask that sanctions be strengthened, and that the Obama administration not be allowed so many waivers to permit other countries to flout the sanctions regime, until Iran actually changes its conduct—not just promises to change it. That is, sanctions should be reduced in the coming months only in exchange for Iran's exporting enriched uranium, warehousing centrifuges, and providing truthful information about the military aspects of its nuclear program.

Finally, Netanyahu will ask that the military option be strengthened, not weakened. Here, Washington's rhetoric matters, but it could do far more to bolster the now-diminished credibility of its threat to use force by carefully leaking information about U.S. military preparations or by positioning forces so that they could strike Iran should it be necessary. But the Israelis may guess that they won't get much here, so a more promising line may be to ask Washington to help them enhance their own capabilities—by providing more bunker-buster bombs and more air refueling tankers. The idea would be to demonstrate that, at least for Israel, all options are in fact on the table, and that the Americans like it that way.

The first three steps could be taken without the approval of the Obama administration—in fact, they are steps meant to limit U.S.

flexibility. The fourth step would require the Obama administration's approval and action. If Israel plays its cards right, it might be able to convince Washington to help with the fourth step by promising to refrain from the first three. That is, Israel could say it can live with the possibility of Iranian cheating and moving closer to a bomb only if its own military option grows stronger.

Israel does retain one option for stymying the negotiations if they appear to be heading for what Israelis would view as a bad deal, one that would allow Iran to escape sanctions and creep closer to a bomb. That is for Israel to attack Iranian nuclear sites. Its ability to do so is already being narrowed considerably by the diplomatic thaw, because it is one thing to bomb Iran when it appears hopelessly recalcitrant and isolated and quite another to bomb it when much of the world—especially the United States—is optimistic about the prospect of talks. A window for an Israeli attack might open up if the talks bogged down and Western negotiators suggested that the Iranians were refusing to compromise, perhaps speculating that the Supreme Leader and the Revolutionary Guards did not want a deal after all. But Rouhani and his foreign minister, Mohammad Javad Zarif, are probably too smart to allow such pessimism to creep into Western ranks.

In short, the Israelis find themselves in a far worse position now than they have been for several years. There was no way for them to avoid this situation other than attacking last year; bombing Iran when Mahmoud Ahmadinejad was president would have been more defensible in the court of global public opinion. Now they must fix bleak smiles to their lips and say that they hope for the best—all the while wringing their hands about the likely terms of the deal. Given that Israel may have little ability to persuade the Western negotiators to be tough, its best path for now is to appeal to Americans, especially in Congress, to refuse to lift sanctions until Iran makes significant concessions.

Here, the Syria episode might actually help Israel, since it increased mistrust about the Obama administration's handling of foreign policy, even among Democrats. Refusing to lift sanctions and adopting tougher rhetoric toward Iran would not be partisan issues. Plenty of Democrats think that those actions are both good politics and good policy.

The Israelis have a difficult task ahead. They do not wish to play the bad cop role in an American game with Iran—and, in fact, the metaphor is misleading. In the good cop/bad cop routine, both officers are on the same team and are carefully coordinating their approaches. In this case, the Israelis fear, the bad cop wants to see the criminals jailed, and the good cop is open to a sweet plea bargain. If that's what the Iranians get, they will sit back and smile while the United States and Israel end up in a bitter argument. ☯

Why Israel Is So Afraid

Iran, the United States, and the Bomb

Ariel Ilan Roth

The Obama administration is hoping that its recent deal with Iran will make the Middle East more stable. But the opposite outcome is at least as likely. For Israel in particular, the deal is a bad omen—not because of what it says about the prospect of Iran obtaining nuclear weapons but because of what many fear it says about the United States' commitment to Israeli security. In addition to believing that the agreement itself is no good, Israelis suspect that the United States' pursuit of it signals the end of deep U.S. involvement in the region, upon which Israel has long relied to overcome isolation. Without the American safety net, Israel could now defy U.S. expectations and attempt to deal with emergent threats preemptively, disproportionately, and entirely unilaterally.

By some estimates, Israel has never been safer. The peace treaty with Egypt, the cornerstone of Israel's security for the last 30 years, survived an uncertain period of Islamist rule in Egypt and is now guarded once more by an Egyptian military government that seems intent on staying put. The peace with Jordan looks as durable as ever, and further to the east, Iraq is decades away from rebuilding

ARIEL ILAN ROTH is the executive director of the Israel Institute in Washington, D.C.

a military strong enough to threaten Israel. Events in Syria are even more fortuitous. Syrian President Bashar al-Assad, stripped of chemical weapons—his poor man's answer to Israel's impressive nuclear arsenal—seems likely to survive his civil war. The Golan Heights, under his control, will presumably remain quiet, and it will be a long time before the Syrian army can credibly threaten Israel.

Despite these objectively good conditions, Israeli Prime Minister Benjamin Netanyahu has taken to the hustings to decry the U.S.-backed interim agreement as a horribly misguided policy that will lead to Iran's eventual emergence as a nuclear power. Israel's reaction should not come as a surprise, since the country's strong opposition to the prospect of any other nuclear power in its region is an established fact. Israeli raids on Iraq in 1981 and Syria in 2007, both of which aimed to destroy nascent nuclear infrastructure, have proved as much. The fact that Israel has not yet launched a similar raid against Iran is likely a reflection of the technological and political challenges—both internal and international—that attacking Iran would entail.

To understand why, one needs to look back. Israel's founding prime minister, David Ben-Gurion, believed that, given Israel's position as a small and regionally unwelcomed Jewish state in the otherwise Muslim region, his country's security required a great-power patron. Although Israel would always have to fight its own battles, he believed, a patron could provide the arms for waging them and the diplomatic resources for protecting the gains resulting from them. Historically, Israel's security policy has been the most restrained when its relationship with its great-power patron was at its most robust. For example, Israel's acceptance of a premature end to the fighting in the Sinai in October 1973 came at the behest of the United States, with whom its ties had never been stronger. So did its restraint in the face of Iraqi Scud missiles in 1991. In both cases, Israeli behavior went against the grain of its preferred policies. In the first, the end of fighting before Israel fully encircled and expelled Egyptian forces from the eastern bank of the Sinai gave Egyptian President Anwar al-Sadat the political victory he sought. In the second, Israel's non-retaliation in the face of Iraqi Scuds arguably encouraged organizations such as Hezbollah, Hamas, and the Palestinian Islamic Jihad to believe that Israel's commitment to bloody retribution, which had been firmly established in the 1950s, was waning.

Contrast Israel's behavior in both of those cases with its policy in May 1967, when Israel felt abandoned by a great-power patron. Following the closing of the Straits of Tiran by Egypt's president, Gamal Abdel al-Nasser, Israel sought the reassurance of its traditional partner France that it would either pressure Egypt itself to open the straits or stand by Israel if the latter sought to reopen the straits on its own. French President Charles de Gaulle, looking to repair France's reputation in the Middle East after the extreme violence of the Algerian civil war, rebuffed the request. With neither the United Kingdom nor the United States offering Israel a place under their defense umbrellas, Israel found itself, according to Golda Meir, who later became its prime minister, hauntingly alone. Israel's response to its sense of profound isolation was a paroxysm of violence that, in the span of six days, transformed the Middle East and created problems for Israel and the rest of the world that remain unresolved today.

The United States' realignment of its foreign policy after the costly wars in Iraq and Afghanistan, in the face of an increasingly powerful China and a weakened economy, threatens to plunge Israel back into those haunting days. Washington needs to recognize that if it is to understand Israel's reaction to the U.S. deal with Iran. The Obama administration maintains that this deal is only an interim agreement and that, should it fail, military options remain on the table, but those claims are quite suspect. Since the invasion of Iraq, the United States has signaled deep reluctance to use force in any circumstances that are likely to cause U.S. casualties or to seriously jeopardize other interests. The United States' tepid participation in Libya was one such signal. Its decision to allow Syria to breach the "red line" on chemical weapons was another.

American calculations are causing unease in Israel. For Israel, its long-term security outlook remains troubling for three reasons. First, the Arab Spring has revealed strong popular tendencies toward Islamist politics in the region, which gives Arab politicians who attempt to ride popular will significantly less inclination to accommodate Israel than the autocrats who preceded them. Such shifting priorities suggest that even the peace that Israel enjoys with Egypt and Jordan may be a thin reed. Israel must prepare for the worst—abrogated peace treaties and sincere popular backing for active opposition to Israel within the Arab world. Second, Israel's ability to deter aggression is eroding. If its deterrent credibility was plotted on a graph, the high point would have been at the end of the 1967 war. Starting with Israel's incomplete victory in 1973, through the decision not to retaliate against Iraq in 1991, and on to Hezbollah and Hamas' success in winning territorial concessions through insurgency, the costs of opposing Israel appear to have decreased. Third, the lack of U.S. resolve on Syria and Iran leaves the impression that the United States is seeking to disentangle from the Middle East as its gaze turns elsewhere. If the United States should, for whatever reason, seek to downgrade its relationship with Israel, it is not clear where Israel would turn for weapons and diplomatic cover. Domestic production of cutting-edge arms is likely beyond Israel's economic (although not technological) means, as the failed effort to produce an Israeli-made fighter in the 1980s demonstrated. Add to that that the chilly reception that Israel receives from most actors in the international system other than the United States and it is clear why Israel is worried.

Some will say that Israel's concerns are overblown and that U.S. support for Israel is unshakable. Indeed, President Barack Obama and Secretary of State John Kerry have been making that very argument for weeks. Israel can be forgiven for taking only cold comfort from these reassurances. In the end, as Lord Palmerston's dictum goes, states have no permanent friends, only interests. To gauge how Israel is likely to react from here on out, the most likely point of insight is from Thucydides' observations on why Sparta initiated its war against Athens. A power in fear of being eclipsed has every incentive to strike first in the hope of delaying its potential downfall.

Since Israeli Prime Minister Benjamin Netanyahu has been threatening action against Iran for years, many see him now as the boy who cried wolf. They believe that Israel would not dare attack Iran in the midst of a U.S. diplomatic gambit. But such observers would do well to remember Sadat, who declared both 1971 and 1972 to be the year of decision against Israel, only to be ridiculed at the years' ends when his armies never left their barracks. Israel made the mistake of dismissing Sadat and received its comeuppance when he finally did attack in 1973. Similarly, no one should assume that the threat of war has passed. The United States' diplomatic engagement with Iran may, ironically, make Israel more likely to attack now, because later could be too late. ☯

www.ingramcontent.com/pod-product-compliance
Lightning Source LLC
Chambersburg PA
CBHW072205270326

41930CB00011B/2540